Font Garden™

A professional collection of 500 fonts
for Windows and Macintosh

Related Titles

If you like this CDROM, you'll enjoy these too!

2000 TrueType Fonts & 5000 Clip Art Images™
A collection of fonts and images by PDSL (Public Domain Shareware Library).

Clip Art Cornucopia™
5000 clip art images to use in your newsletters, greeting cards, and more.

Raytrace! The Official POV-RAY CDROM
A beautiful collection of computer generated images, plus programs to create your own images.

Visions
500 royalty-free photographs from Preferred Stock Photo Agency.

Travel Adventure
395 royalty-free photographs from around the world, color booklet of contact sheets included.

Fractal Frenzy
1000's of fractal images including examples of all the major types from Mandelbrot to Zexpe.

Fractal Frenzy 2
A collection of 2127 fractal images by eight renowned artists.

GIFs Galore
600 megabytes of GIF images in thirty-nine categories from abstract art to Vietnam.

All of these titles are available through your local bookstore or software retailer. For more information call +1-510-674-0783.

Font Garden™

A professional collection of 500 fonts for Windows and Macintosh

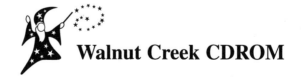 **Walnut Creek CDROM**

Font Garden™
Published by Walnut Creek CDROM
Suite 260, 1547 Palos Verdes Mall,
Walnut Creek CA 94596 USA
• Sales +1-510 674-0783 • Tech support +1-510 603-1234
• Fax +1 510 674-0821 • info@cdrom.com

Copyright © 1995 Walnut Creek CDROM
Cover designer: Ellen Y. Hsu

Printed in the United States of America

0 9 8 7 6 5 4 3 2 1

ISBN 1-57176-096-2

Table of Contents

Acknowledgments

Please remember that although you own this disc, you do not own all of the programs and fonts recorded on it. Many fonts and programs on this disc are shareware. You are free to try each program for a limited time. If you are satisfied and want to continue to use the program, you should register it by sending a specified amount of money directly to the author of the program. Often the author will send you the most up-to-date version of the program and a printed manual. Please check the individual files for specific information.

Also note that the font names used by the authors of the fonts on this disc may sometimes be similar to certain commercial (not public domain or shareware) fonts. Please be aware that the fonts on this disc may differ considerably from these commercial versions.

How to Use this CDROM and book

To use this book:

This book is a reference guide to the Font Garden™ CDROM. It displays the basic characters of each font found on the disc. Most of the fonts on this disc come in files compatible with Windows and Macintosh, in both Type 1 PostScript and TrueType formats. Organized in alphabetical order, the name of each font appears above the character display. To find where the font files are located on the disc, simply look in the subdirectories on the CDROM labeled "Mac TrueType Font" and "Mac Type 1 Fonts" for fonts in Macintosh format, or "TTF" and "Type 1" for fonts in Windows format. For Windows users, the corresponding file name of each font format is also listed directly underneath the character display on each page.

Font Installation

Installing Fonts with a Macintosh:

The fonts for use under a Macintosh system are located in two folders, "Mac TrueType Fonts" and "Mac Type 1 Fonts." To install any of the fonts therein, simply drag the font to your System Folder.

MSDOS Quick Start:

To use this disc with the MSDOS prompt, first change drives to your CDROM drive. Then type *View* in the root directory of the CDROM drive and press *Enter*.

    Example: C: \> D:
           D: \> *View*

The *View* program will display a listing of the CDROM's

subdirectories and their descriptions. Use the cursor (arrow) keys to move the highlight bar up and down the screen. After highlighting the desired subdirectory, press **Enter** to change to that subdirectory. The **View** program will then display a list of files within that particular subdirectory. To view or run any of these files, use the cursor (arrow) keys to highlight the desired file and press **Enter**. To copy a particular file, press the **C** key. To return to the subdirectory listing, press the **Escape** key. Pressing **?** will display a help screen.

Please consult \DOCS\VIEW.DOC for a complete explanation on all of the features of the **View** program.

Installing the FONTVIEW.EXE program for Windows:

The FONTVIEW.EXE program allows you to easily view and add the TrueType fonts from the CDROM into your Windows setup. To install the FONTVIEW.EXE program:

1. Start up Windows.

2. From the Windows Program Manager, choose **Run** from the File menu.

3. In the dialog box, type **D:\Setup**. (If the D: drive is not your CDROM drive, change it to the appropriate CDROM drive letter.)

This will create a program group for this disc, as well as icons for the programs that can be run directly from the CDROM.

Manually installing TrueType Fonts into Windows:

1. While at the MSDOS prompt, change to your CDROM drive and type **View** in the root directory of the CDROM drive, then press **Enter**.

Example: C: \> D:

D: \> *View*

If your CDROM drive is not the D: drive, substitute your CDROM drive letter for D:.

2. Within the *View* program, use the cursor (arrow) keys to move the highlight bar up and down. Choose the TrueType Fonts directory, and press *Enter*.

3. Select which category you wish to view by moving the highlight bar up and down, and then pressing *Enter*. You may go back to the previous menu by pressing the *Escape* key.

4. While in the TrueType fonts categories, use the highlight bar to choose a font. Press *Enter* to copy the font onto your hard drive.

5. At the Destination prompt, type the location of your Windows System Directory. On non-customized systems, this would normally be *C:\WINDOWS\SYSTEM*. This will copy the highlighted TrueType font into your Windows System Directory.

6. Install as many fonts as you would like this way, then press the *Escape* key until you exit back to the MSDOS prompt.

7. Start up Windows, if you are not already using it.

8. In the Control Panel window (usually located within the Main program group), choose the *Fonts* icon. The Fonts dialog box appears.

9. Choose the *Add* button.

10. Open the Drives list, and then select the drive that contains your Windows directory, for example *C:\Windows*. In the Directories box select the Windows directory, then select the System Directory to which the fonts were copied earlier in

Step 5.

11. From the List of Fonts box, select the fonts you want to add by clicking on it once. You can extend the selection to add several fonts at once. Or, to add every font in the list, choose the *Select All* button.

12. Choose the *OK* button.

For more information on using TrueType fonts with Windows, please consult your Microsoft Windows User's Guide.

To Remove TrueType Fonts from Windows:

1. In the Control Panel window (usually located within the Main program group), choose the *Fonts* icon. The Fonts dialog box appears.

2. From the Installed Fonts list, select the font you want to remove by clicking on it once. Then choose the *Remove* button. The Remove Font window will appear.

3. If you want to delete the font files from your disk in addition to removing the fonts from memory, select the Delete Font File From Disc check box. Then choose the *Yes* button. Or, if you are removing several fonts at once, choose the *Yes To All* button.

Using Type 1 PostScript Fonts under Windows:

Windows does not natively support PostScript fonts. The commercial product Adobe Type Manager will allow you to use PostScript fonts under Windows. You can purchase Adobe Type Manager separately.

ABCDEFGHIJKLMNO
PQRSTUVWXYZ
abcdefghijklmnopqrstu
vwxyz
0123456789&$.,:;!?

Type 1 filename: activa__.afm   TrueType filename: activa__.ttf

Activa Bold

ABCDEFGHIJKLMN
OPQRSTUVWXYZ
abcdefghijklmnopqrs
tuvwxyz
0123456789&$.,:;!?

Type 1 filename: activa_b.afm   TrueType filename: activa_b.ttf

Aarcover Plain

ABCDEFGHIJKLMNOP
QRSTUVWXYZ

ABCDEFGHIJKLMNOPQRSTUVW
XYZ
0123456789$.,:;!?

Type 1 filename: aarco1__.afm   TrueType filename: aarco1__.ttf

AdineKirnberg Script

ABCDEFGHIJKLM
NOPQRSTUVWXYZ

abcdefghijklmnopqrstuvwxyz

0123456789&.,:;!?

Type 1 filename: adks____.afm   TrueType filename: adks____.ttf

Adjutant Normal

ABCDEFGHIJKLMNOPQ
RSTUVWXYZ
abcdefghijklmnopq
rstuvwxyz
0123456789&$.,:;!?

Type 1 fielname: adjutant.afm   TrueType filename: adjutant.ttf

ABCDEFGHIJKLMNOPQRS TUVWXYZ
abcdefghijklmnopqrstuvwxyz
0123456789&$.,:;!?

Type 1 filename: albatros.afm   TrueType filename: albatros.ttf

———— **Alex Antiqua Book** ————

ABCDEFGHIJKLMNO PQRSTUVWXYZ
abcdefghijklmnopqrstuv
wxyz
0123456789&$.,:;!?

Type 1 filename: aann____.afm   TrueType filename: aann____.ttf

Alexandria

ABCDEFGHIJKLMNOPQRST
UVWXYZ
abcdefghijklmnopqrstuvw
xyz
0123456789G$.,:;1?

Type 1 filename: alexan__.afm   TrueType filename: alexan__.ttf

Alpine Medium

ABCDEFGHIJKLMNOP
QRSTUVWXYZ
abcdefghijklmnopqrstuvw
xyz
0123456789&$.,:;!?

Type 1 filename: alpine__.afm   TrueType filename: alpine__.ttf

ABCDEFGHIJKLMNOPQRSTU
VWXYZ

ABCDEFGHIJKLMNOPQRSTUVWXYZ
0123456789&$.,:;!?

Type 1 filename: ambro___.afm   TrueType filename: ambro___.ttf

Amerton Outline

ABCDEFGHIJKLMNOP
QRSTUVWXYZ
abcdefghijklmnopqrstuv
wxyz
0123456789&$.,:;!?

Type 1 filename: amerto__.afm   TrueType filename: amerto__.ttf

Amerton Outline Italic

ABCDEFGHIJKLMNOP
QRSTUVWXYZ
abcdefghijklmnopqrstuv
wxyz
0123456789&$.,:;!?

Type 1 filename: amerto_i.afm   TrueType filename: amerto_i.ttf

Andromeda

PBCDEFGHIJKLMNOPQRSTU
VWXYZ

abcdefghijklmnopqrstuvwxyz
0123456789&$.,:;!?

Type 1 filename: andrmeda.afm   TrueType filename: andrmeda.ttf

Aneirin Medium

ABCDEFGHIJKL
MNOPQRSTUVW
XYZ

Type 1 filename: aneirin_.afm   TrueType filename: aneirin_.ttf

Animals Medium

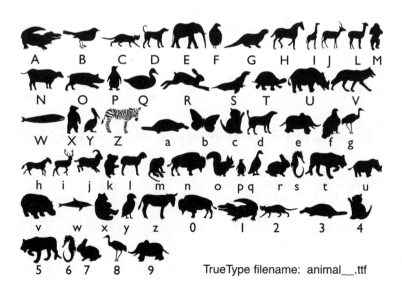

A B C D E F G H I J L M
N O P Q R S T U V
W X Y Z a b c d e f g
h i j k l m n o p q r s t u
v w x y z 0 1 2 3 4
5 6 7 8 9

TrueType filename: animal__.ttf

8

ABCDEFGHIJKLMNOP
QRSTUVWXYZ
abcdefghijklmnopqrs
tuvwxyz
0123456789$.,:;!?

Type 1 filename: anson___.afm   TrueType filename: anson___.ttf

ABCDEFGHIJKLMNOP
QRSTUVWXYZ
abcdefghijklmnopqrst
uvwxyz
0123456789&$.,:;!?

Type 1 filename: arctic__.afm   TrueType filename: arctic__.ttf

Arenski-Lengyar Italic —————

CDEFGHIJKLM
NOPQRSTUVWXYZ
abcdefghijklmnopqrstuvw
xyz
0123456789&$.,:;!?

Type 1 filename: arenski_.afm   TrueType filename: arenski_.ttf

————— # Ariston Medium Italic —————

ABCDEFGHIJKLM
NOPQRSTUVWXYZ
abcdefghijklmnopqrstu
vwxyz
0123456789&$.,:;!?

Type 1 filename: aristo_i.afm   TrueType filename: aristo_i.ttf

Ariston Extra Bold Italic

ABCDEFGHIJKLMN
OPQRSTUVWXYZ
abcdefghijklmnopqrstu
vwxyz
12345678&$.,:;!?

Type 1 filename: aristobi.afm   TrueType filename: aristobi.ttf

Artlookin

ABCDEFGHIJKL
MNOPQRSTUVW
XYZ
ABCDEFGHIJKLMNO
PQRSTUVWXYZ
0123456789&$.,:;!?

Type 1 filename: artloo__.afm   TrueType filename: artloo__.ttf

Artlookin Italic

ABCDEFGHIJKL
MNOPQRSTUVW
XYZ
ABCDEFGHIJKLMNO
PQRSTUVWXYZ
0123456789&$.,;:'!?

Type 1 filename: artloo_i.afm   TrueType filename: artloo_i.ttf

Artlookin Bold

ABCDEFGHIJKLM
NOPQRSTUVWXYZ
ABCDEFGHIJKLMNO
PQRSTUVWXYZ
0123456789&$.,;:'!?

Type 1 filename: artloo_b.afm   TrueType filename: artloo_b.ttf

Ashley

ABCDEFGHIJKLMNOPQRS
TUVWXYZ
abcdefghijklmnopqrstuv
wxyz
0123456789$.,:;!?

Type 1 filename: ashley__.afm   TrueType filename: ashley__.ttf

Athletic

ABCDEFGHIJKLMN
OPQRSTUVWXYZ
ABCDEFGHIJKLMNOPQRST
UVWXYZ
0123456789$.,:;!?

Type 1 filename: athletic.afm   TrueType filename: athletic.ttf

ABCDEFGHIJKLMN
OPQRSTUVWXYZ

Type 1 and TrueType format not available for Windows

B

Balsam

$\mathcal{ABCDEFGHIJKLMNOPQ}$
$\mathcal{RSTUVWXYZ}$
abcdefghijklmnopqrstuvwxyz
0123456789&$..:;!?

Type 1 filename: balsam__.afm   TrueType filename: balsam__.ttf

Beachman Script

$\mathcal{ABCDEFGHIJKLMNO}$
$\mathcal{PQRSTUVWXYZ}$
abcd ef ghijklmnopqrstuvwxyz
0123456789.,:;!?

Type 1 filename: beachman.afm   TrueType filename: beachman.ttf

ABCDEFGHIJKLMNOP
QRSTUVWXYZ
abcdefghijklmnopqr
stuvwxyz
0123456789&$.,:;!?

Type 1 filename: ble_____.afm   TrueType filename: ble_____.ttf

--- **Beffle** ---

ABCDEFGHIJKLM
NOPQRSTUVW
XYZ

Type 1 filename: beffle__.afm   TrueType filename: beffle__.ttf

Bell Bottom

ABCDEFGHIJKLMNOPQRS
TUVWXYZ
abcdefghijklmnopqrstuv
wxyz
0123456789&$.,:;!?

Type 1 filename: bebl____.afm   TrueType filename: bebl____.ttf

Benjamin Capitals

ABCDEFGHIJKLM
NOPQRSTUVW
XYZ

ABCDEFGHIJKLMNOPQRST
UVWXYZ

Type 1 filename: bec_____.afm   TrueType filename: bec_____.ttf

— Bikly Bold —

Bikly Bold

ABCDEFGHIJKLMNO
PQRSTUVWXYZ

ABCDEFGHIJKLMNOPQRSTUVW

XYZ

0123456789&$.,::!?

Type 1 filename: biklybld.afm   TrueType filename: biklybld.ttf

Bills Dingbats

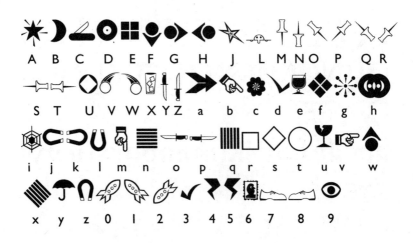

Type 1 filename: billsdin.afm   TrueType filename: billsdin.ttf

ABCDEFGHIJKLMNOPQRSTUV
WXYZ

ABCDEFGHIJKLMNOPQRSTUVWXYZ
0123456789.,:;!?

Type 1 filename: bladder2.afm   TrueType filename: bladder2.ttf

Black Chancery

ABCDEFGHIJKL
MNOPQRSTUVW
XYZ
abcdefghijklmnopqrstuvw
xyz
0123456789&$.,:;!?

Type 1 filename: blackcha.afm   TrueType filename: blackcha.ttf

ABCDEFGHIJKLMN
OPQRSTUVWXYZ
abcdefghijklmnopqrstuv
wxyz
0123456789&$.,:;!?

Type 1 filename: blkforst.afm   TrueType filename: blkforst.ttf

Blockboys

ABCDEFGHIJKLMN
OPQRSTUVWXYZ
ABCDEFGHIJKLMN
OPQRSTUVWXYZ
0123456789&$.,
:;!?

Type 1 filename: blockboy.afm   TrueType filename: blockboy.ttf

ABCDEFGHIJKLMNOPQ
RSTUVWXYZ
abcdefghijklmnopqrstu
vwxyz
0123456789&$.,:;!?

Type 1 filename: bodacius.afm   TrueType filename: bodacius.ttf

—————————————— **BODIDLY Bold** ——————————————

ABCDEFGHIJKLM
NOPQRSTUVW
XYZ
abcdefghijklmnopq
rstuvwxyz
0123456789&$.,:;!?

Type 1 filename: bodidlyb.afm   TrueType filename: bodidlyb.ttf

Bodidly Condensed

ABCDEFGHIJKLMNOPQRSTUVW
XYZ
abcdefghijklmnopqrstuvwxyz
0123456789&$.,:;!?

Type 1 filename: bodidlyc.afm   TrueType filename: bodidlyc.ttf

Bone Black Medium

ABCDEFGHIJKLMNOPQRS
TUVWXYZ
abcdefghijklmnopqrstuv
wxyz
0123456789&$.,:;!?

Type 1 filename: boneblak.afm   TrueType filename: boneblak.ttf

ABCDEFGHIJKLMN OPQRSTUVWXYZ

abcdefghijklmnopqrstuv wxyz

0123456789&$.,:;!?

Type 1 filename: boston__.afm   TrueType filename: boston__.ttf

Boston Italic

ABCDEFGHIJKLMNOP QRSTUVWXYZ

abcdefghijklmnopqrstu vwxyz

0123456789&$.,:;!?

Type 1 filename: boston_i.afm   TrueType filename: boston_i.ttf

ABCDEFGHIJKLMN OPQRSTUVWXYZ abcdefghijklmnopqrs tuvwxyz 0123456789&$.,:;!?

Type 1 filename: boston_b.afm   TrueType filename: boston_b.ttf

— Boston Bold Italic —

ABCDEFGHIJKLMNO PQRSTUVWXYZ abcdefghijklmnopqrst uvwxyz 0123456789&$.,:;!?

Type 1 filename: bostonbi.afm   TrueType filename: bostonbi.ttf

Braille

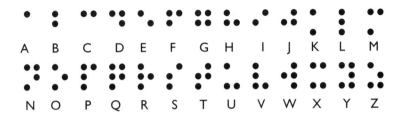

A B C D E F G H I J K L M

N O P Q R S T U V W X Y Z

Type 1 filename: brf_____.afm   TrueType filename: brf_____.ttf

Brassfield Italic

ABCDEFGHIJKLMNOPQ
RSTUVWXYZ
abcdefghijklmnopqrstu
vwxyz
0123456789&$.,:;!?

Type 1 filename: brassfld.afm   TrueType filename: brassfld.ttf

ABCDEFGHIJKLMNO
PQRSTUVWXYZ
abcdefghijklmnopq
rstuvwxyz

Type 1 filename: buccanee.afm   TrueType filename: buccanee.ttf

Bucephalus

ABCDEFGHIJKLMN
OP2RSTUVWXYZ
abcdefghijklmnopqrst
uvwxyz
0123456789:;!?

Type 1 filename: buc_____.afm

ABCDEFGHIJKLMNOPQRSTU
VWXYZ

ABCDEFGHIJKLMNOPQRSTUVWXYZ

0123456789$.,:;!?

TrueType filename: bujardet.ttf

Burgundian

ABCDEFGHIJKL
MNOPQRSTUV
WXYZ

0123456789.,:;!?

Type 1 and TrueType format not available for Windows

Cairo

**ABCDEFGHIJKLMNOP
QRSTUVWXYZ
abcdefghijklmnopqrstu
vwxyz
0123456789&$.,:;!?**

Type 1 filename: cairo____.afm   TrueType filename: cairo____.ttf

ABCDEFGHIJKLMNO
PQRSTUVWXYZ
0123456789&,

Type 1 filename: caitlyn_.afm   TrueType filename: caitlyn_.ttf

Caligula

ABCDEFGHIJKLMNO
PQRSTUVWXYZ
abcdefghijklmnopqrstuv
wxyz
0123456789&$.,:;!?

Type 1 filename: calig___.afm   TrueType filename: calig___.ttf

ABCDEFGHIJKLM
NOPQRSTUVWXYZ
abcdefghijklmnopqrst
uvwxyz
0123456789&$.,:;!?

Type 1 filename: camberic.afm   TrueType filename: camberic.ttf

Cambridge Normal

ABCDEFGHIJKLMNOPQRST
UVWXYZ
abcdefghijklmnopqrstuvwxyz
0123456789&$.,:;!?

Type 1 filename: cambridg.afm   TrueType filename: cambridg.ttf

Canaith

ABCDEFGHIJKLMNOPQRS
TUVWXYZ
abcdefghijklmnopqrstuvw
xyz
0123456789&$.,:;!?

Type 1 filename: canaith_.afm   TrueType filename: canaith_.ttf

Caraway Bold

ABCDEFGHIJKLMNO
PQRSTUVWXYZ
abcdefghijklmnopqrs
tuvwxyz
0123456789&$.,:;!?

Type 1 filename: cab____.afm   TrueType filename: cab____.ttf

ABCDEFGHIJKLMNOP
QRSTUVWXYZ
abcdefghijklmnopqrstuv
wxyz
0123456789&$.,:;!?

Type 1 filename: cardif__.afm   TrueType filename: cardif__.ttf

Cardiff Italic

ABCDEFGHIJKLMNOP
QRSTUVWXYZ
abcdefghijklmnopqrstuv
wxyz
0123456789&$.,:;!?

Type 1 filename: cardif_i.afm   TrueType filename: cardif_i.ttf

ABCDEFGHIJKLMNO
PQRSTUVWXYZ
abcdefghijklmnopqrst
uvwxyz
0123456789&$.,:;!?

Type 1 filename: cardif_b.afm   TrueType filename: cardif_b.ttf

Cardiff Bold Italic

ABCDEFGHIJKLMNO
PQRSTUVWXYZ
abcdefghijklmnopqrstuv
wxyz
0123456789&$.,:;!?

Type 1 filename: cardifbi.afm   TrueType filename: cardifbi.ttf

ABCDEFGHIJKLMNOP
QRSTUVWXYZ

ABCDEFGHIJKLMNOPQRSTUVW
XYZ
0123456789&$.,:;!?

Type 1 filename: carolu__.afm   TrueType filename: carolu__.ttf

———————— **Carolus Itlaic** ————————

ABCDEFGHIJKLMNOP
QRSTUVWXYZ
0123456789&$.,:;!?

Type 1 filename: carolu_i.afm   TrueType filename: carolu_i.ttf

Carrick Capitals

ABCDEFGHIJKLMNO

PQRSTUVWXYZ

ABCDEFGHIJKLMNOPQRSTUV

WXYZ

Type 1 filename: cac_____.afm   TrueType filename: cac_____.ttf

Cartwright

ABCDEFGHIJKLMNOPQRSTUVWXYZ

abcdefghijklmnopqrstuvwxyz

0123456789&$.,:;!?

Type 1 filename: cartwri_.afm   TrueType filename: cartwri_.ttf

ABCDEFGHIJKLMNOPQRST
UVWXYZ
abcdefghijklmnopqrstuvw
xyz
0123456789&$.,:;1?

Type 1 filename: cascade_.afm   TrueType filename: cascade_.ttf

Casting

ABCDEFGHIJKLMNOPQRSTUVWXY
Z0123456789&$.,:;!?

Type 1 filename: casting_.afm   TrueType filename: casting_.ttf

ABCDEFGHIJKLMNOPQR
STUVWXYZ

ABCDEFGHIJKLMNOPQRSTUV
WXYZ
0123456789&$.,:;!?

Type 1 filename: cavemann.afm   TrueType filename: cavemann.ttf

Channels

ABCDEFGHIJKLMNOPQRSTU
VWXYZ
abcdefghijklmnopqrstuvwxyz
0123456789.,:;?

Type 1 filename: channels.afm   TrueType filename: channels.ttf

ABCDEFGHIJKLMN
OPQRSTUVWXYZ
abcdefghijKlmnopqrst
uvwxyz
0123456789&$.,:;!?

Type 1 filename: charchan.afm   TrueType filename: charchan.ttf

Chasline Medium

ABCDEFGHIJKLMNOPQRSTUVWXYZ

abcdefghijklmnopqrstuvwxyz

0123456789&$.,:;!?

Type 1 filename: chasline.afm   TrueType filename: chasline.ttf

Cheq Medium

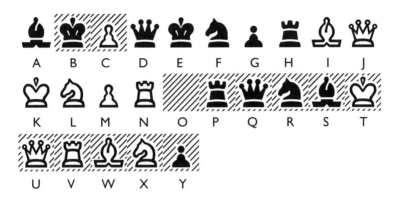

A B C D E F G H I J

K L M N O P Q R S T

U V W X Y

Type 1 filename: cheq____.afm   TrueType filename: cheq____.ttf

Cherokee

iᏁᎶᏉᎡᎤᎣᏫᎨᎿᏒᎡᏢᏇᎢᏟᏜ

A B C D E F G H I J K L M N

ᏚᏇᎷᎹᎬ᎞ᎿᎳᏂᏣᎦᏊᏓ

O P Q R S T U V W X Y Z

ᎠᏩᏴᎸᏖ ᏭᏤᎤᏧᎢᏞᏝᎣ

a b c d e f g h i j k l m n

ᏙᏤᏨᏟᏕᏒᏒᏬᎶᎠᎹᏃᎻ

o p q r s t u v w x y z

ᎮᏉᎶᎤᏐᎭᎴᏫᏏᏚᎻᎷᏔᎻᎯᎭᏍ.,:;?

1 2 3 4 5 6 7 8 9 0 & $

Type 1 filename: cherokee.afm   TrueType filename: cherokee.ttf

ABCDEFGHIJKLMNOP
QRSTUVWXYZ
abcdefghijklmnopqrstu
vwxyz
0123456789&$.,:;!?

Type 1 filename: chessla_.afm   TrueType filename: chessla_.ttf

── **Chopin Open Face** ──

ABCDEFGHIJKLMN
OPQRSTUVWXYZ
abcdefghijklmnopqrstuvw
xyz
0123456789&$.,:;!?

Type 1 filename: chof____.afm   TrueType filename: chof____.ttf

ABCDEFGHIJKLMN
OPQRSTUVWXYZ

abcdefghijklmnopqrstuvwxyz

0123456789& $.,:;!?

Type 1 filename: ci_____.afm   TrueType filename: ci_____.ttf

Clarita Italc

ABCDEFGHIJKLMN
OPQRSTUVW XYZ
abcdefghijk lm nopq
rstuv w xy z
0123456789 & $.,:;!?

Type 1 filename: clarita_.afm   TrueType filename: clarita_.ttf

ABCDEFGHIJKLMN
OPQRSTUVWXYZ
abcdefghijk lm nopqr
stuvw xyz
0123456789&$.,:;!?

Type 1 filename: class__r.afm   TrueType filename: class__r.ttf

ABCDEFGHIJKLMN
OPQRSTUVWXYZ
abcdefghijk lm nopq
rstuvw xyz
0123456789 &$.,:;!?

Type 1 filename: class_mi.afm   TrueType filename: class_mi.ttf

ABCDEFGHIJKLMNO
PQRSTUVWXYZ
abcdefg hijklmnopqr
stuvwxyz
0123456789&$.,:;!?

Type 1 filename: class__h.afm   TrueType filename: class__h.ttf

Cloister Black

ABCDEFGHIJKLMNO
PQRSTUVWXYZ
abcdefghijklmnopqrstuvwxyz
0123456789&$.,:;!?

Type 1 filename: cloister.afm   TrueType filename: cloister.ttf

Code 39 Medium

A B C D E F G H I J K L M N O P Q R

S T U V W X Y Z

0 1 2 3 4 5 6 7 8 9

Type 1 filename: code-39_.afm   TrueType filename: code-39_.ttf

Coliseo

ABCDEFGHIJKLMN
OPQRSTUVWXYZ
abcdefghijklm
nopqrstuvwxyz
0123456789&$.,:;!?

Type 1 filename: coliseo_.afm   TrueType filename: coliseo_.ttf

Colton Gothic

𝔄𝔅ℭ𝔇𝔈𝔉𝔊ℌℑ𝔍𝔎𝔏𝔐𝔑

𝔒𝔓𝔔ℜ𝔖𝔗𝔘𝔙𝔚𝔛𝔜ℨ

abcdefghijklmnopqrstuvwxyz

0123456789&$.,:;!?

Type 1 filename: colton__.afm   TrueType filename: colton__.ttf

Comics Cartoon

ABCDEFGHIJKLMN

OPQRSTUVWXYZ

ABCDEFGHIJKLMNOPQRS

TUVWXYZ

0123456789&$:;!?

Type 1 filename: comics__.afm   TrueType filename: comics__.ttf

CommScript TT

ABCDEFGHIJKLMN
OPQRSTUVWXYZ
abcdefghijklmnopqrstuvw
xyz
0123456789&$.,:;!?

Type 1 filename: comsc___.afm   TrueType filename: comsc___.ttf

Cookie Italic

ABCDEFGHIJKLMN
OPQRSTUVWXYZ
abcdefghijklmnopq
rstuvwxyz
0123456789&$.,:;!?

Type 1 filename: cookie_i.afm   TrueType filename: cookie_i.ttf

ABCDEFGHIJKLM NOPQRSTUVWXY Zabcdefghijklmno pqrstuvwxyz 0123456789&$.,:;!?

Type 1 filename: cooper_i.afm   TrueType filename: cooper__.ttf

Cooper Black Italic

ABCDEFGHIJKLMN OPQRSTUVWXYZ abcdefghijklmnopq rstuvwxyz 0123456789&$.,:;!?

TrueType filename: cooper_i.ttf

ABCDEFGHIJKLMN
OPQRSTUVW XYZ
abcdefgh ijk lm nopqr
stuvw xy z
0123456789&$.,:;!?

Type 1 filename: cordel__.afm   TrueType filename: cordel__.ttf

Cordella Italic

ABCDEFGHIJKLMN
OPQRSTUVW XYZ
abcdefghijk lm nopq
rstuvw xyz
0123456789 &$.,:;!?

Type 1 filename: cordel_i.afm   TrueType filename: cordel_i.ttf

ABCDEFGHIJKLMN
OPQRSTUVWXYZ
abcdefghijklmnopq
rstuvwxyz
0123456789&$.,:;!?

Type 1 filename: cordelhy.afm   TrueType filename: cordelhy.ttf

Type 1 filename: courthan.afm

Crackling Fire

ABCDEFGHIJKLMNOPQRS
TUVWXYZ

ABCDEFGHIJKLMNOPQRSTUVWXYZ
.,:;!?

Type 1 filename: crf_____.afm   TrueType filename: crf_____.ttf

Creedmore

ABCDEFGHIJKLMNOPQRSTUV
WXYZ

abcdefghijklmnopqrstuvwxyz
0123456789&$.,;:!?

Type 1 filename: creedmor.afm   TrueType filename: creedmor.ttf

Crillee

ABCDEFGHIJKLMNO
PQRSTUVWXYZ
abcdefghijklmnopqr
stuvwxyz
0123456789&$.,:;!?

Type 1 filename: crillee_.afm   TrueType filename: crillee_.ttf

CSD-Block Bold

ABCDEFGHIJKLMNOPQRSTUV
WXYZ
abcdefghijklmnopqrstuvw
xyz
0123456789&$.,:;!?

Type 1 filename: csdblock.afm   TrueType filename: csdblock.ttf

CSD-Chalk

ABCDEFGHIJKLMNOPQRS
TUVWXYZ
abcdefghijklmnopqrstuvwxyz
0123456789&$.,:;!?

Type 1 filename: csdchalk.afm   TrueType filename: csdchalk.ttf

CSD-Jersey

ABCDEFGHIJKLMNOP
QRSTUVWXYZ
ABCDEFGHIJKLMNOPQRSTUV
WXYZ
0123456789&$.,:;!?

Type 1 filename: csdjersy.afm   TrueType filename: csdjersy.ttf

Cuneifont Light

ABCDEFGHIJKLMNOPQRST
UVWXYZ
abcdefghijklmnopqrs
tuvwxyz
0123456789&$.,:;!?

Type 1 filename: cunei___.afm   TrueType filename: cunei___.ttf

Cuneiform Medium

ABCDEFGHIJKLMNOPQ
RSTUVWXYZ
abcdefghijklmnopqrst
uvwxyz
0123456789&$.,:;!?

Type 1 filename: cuneifrm.afm   TrueType filename: cuneifrm.ttf

Cursive Elegant Italic

ABCDEFGHIJK
LMNOPQRSTUV
WXYZ
abcdefghijklmnopqrstu
vwxyz
0123456789&$.,:;!?

Type 1 filename: cursive_.afm   TrueType filename: cursive_.ttf

Cyrillic

ФИСВУАПРШОЛДЬТIЩ
A B C D E F G H I J K L M N O
ЗЙКЫЕГМЦЧНЯ
P Q R S T U V W X Y Z
фисвуапршолдьтiщзйкые
a b c d e f g h i j k l m n o p q r s t
ГМЦЧНЯ
u v w x y z
0123456789

Type 1 filename: cyril___.afm   TrueType filename: cyril___.ttf

Cyrillic Italic

ФИСВУАПРШОЛДЬТ
A B C D E F G H I J K L M N

ЩЗЙКЫЕГМЦЧНЯ
O P Q R S T U V W X Y Z

фисвуапршолдьтщзйк
a b c d e f g h i j k l m n o p q r

ыегмцчня
s t u v w x y z

0123456789

Type 1 filename: cyril__i.afm   TrueType filename: cyril__i.ttf

Cyrillic Bold

ФИСВУАПРШОЛДЬТІЩ
A B C D E F G H I J K L M N O

ЗЙКЫЕГМЦЧНЯ
P Q R S T U V W X Y Z

фисвуапршолдьтщзйк
a b c d e f g h i j k l m n o p q r

ыегмцчня
s t u v w x y z

0123456789

Type 1 filename: cyril__b.afm   TrueType filename: cyril__b.ttf

ФИСВУ АПРШОЛ ДЬТ
A B C D E F G H I J K L M N

ЩЗЙКЫЕГМЦЧНЯ
O P Q R S T U V W X Y Z

фисвуапршолдьтщ
a b c d e f g h i j k l m n o

зйкыегмцчня
p q r s t u v w x y z

0123456789

Type 1 filename: cyril_bi.afm   TrueType filename: cyril_bi.ttf

Davy's Big Key Capitals

| A | B | C | D | E | F | G | H | I | J | K | L | M | N |

| O | P | Q | R | S | T | U | V | W | X | Y | Z |

| ALT | RETURN | CAPS LOCK | PRINT SCREEN | ENTER | INS | SCROLL LOCK |

| HOME | ↑ | ← | ↓ | → | DELETE | BACKSPACE |

| OPTION | PAUSE | SHIFT | PAGE DOWN | ESC | TAB |

| END | CONTROL | HELP | ⌘ | DEL | 🍎 |

| 0 | 1 | 2 | 3 | 4 | 5 | 6 | 7 | 8 | 9 | & | $ | . | , |

| : | ; | ! | ? |

Type 1 filename: dabkc___.afm   TrueType filename: dabkc___.ttf

---

Daytona Medium

ABCDEFGHIJKLMNO
PQRSTUVWXYZ
abcdefghijklmnopqrs
tuvwxyz
0123456789&$.,:;!?

Type 1 filename: daytona_.afm   TrueType filename: daytona_.ttf

ABCDEFGHIJKLMNOP
QRSTUVWXYZ
abcdefghijklmnopqr
stuvwxyz
0123456789&$.,:;!?

Type 1 filename: de_____.afm   TrueType filename: de_____.ttf

──────── **Delegate** ────────

ABCDEFGHIJKLMNO
PQRSTUVWXYZ
abcdefghijklmno
pqrstuvwxyz
0123456789&$.,:;!?

TrueType filename: delegate.ttf

ABCDEFGHIJKLMNOPQRSTU VWXYZ

ABCDEFGHIJKLMNOPQRSTUVWXYZ
0123456789&$.,:;!?

Type 1 filename: deusex__.afm   TrueType filename: deusex__.ttf

Devandra

ABCDEFGHIJKLMNO PQRSTUVWXYZ

ABCDEFGHIJKLMNOPQRSTUVW
XYZ
0123456789&$.,:;!?

Type 1 filename: devandra.afm

ABCDEFGHIJKLMNOPQRSTU
VWXYZ

abcdefghijklmnopqrstuvwxyz

0123456789&$.,:;!?

Type 1 filename: diego1__.afm   TrueType filename: diego1__.ttf

Dijkstra Medium

ABCDEFGHIJKLMNOPQR
STUVWXYZ

abcdefghijklmnopqrstuvwxyz
0123456789&$.,:;!?

Type 1 filename: dijkstra.afm   TrueType filename: dijkstra.ttf

ABCDEFGHIJKLMNOPQRSTUVWXYZ
ABCDEFGHIJKLMNOPQRSTUVWXYZ
0123456789&.,:;?

Type 1 filename: diner_fa.afm   TrueType filename: diner_fa.ttf

──────── **Diner-Obese** ────────

ABCDEFGHIJKLMNOPQRSTUVWXYZ
ABCDEFGHIJKLMNOPQRSTUVWXYZ
0123456789&.,:;!?

Type 1 filename: diner_ob.afm   TrueType filename: diner_ob.ttf

Diner-Regular

ABCDEFGHIJKLMNOPQRSTUVWXYZ

ABCDEFGHIJKLMNOPQRSTUVWXYZ

0123456789&.,:;!?

Type 1 filename: diner___.afm   TrueType filename: diner___.ttf

Diner-Skinny

ABCDEFGHIJKLMNOPQRSTUVWXYZ

ABCDEFGHIJKLMNOPQRSTUVWXYZ

0123456789&.,:;!?

Type 1 filename: diner_sk.afm

Dolmen Medium

ABCDEFGHIJKLMNO
PQRSTUVWXYZ
abcdefghijklmnop
qrstuvwxyz
0123456789&$.,:;!

Type 1 filename: dolmen__.afm   TrueType filename: dolmen__.ttf

Donte

ABCDEFGHIJKLMNOP
QRSTUVWXYZ
abcdefghijklmnopqrstuv
wxyz
0123456789&$.,:;!?

Type 1 filename: donte___.afm   TrueType filename: donte___.ttf

Dor Regular

קצפסנמלכף יטזוהדגבשששלדדוּ

A B C D E F G H I J K L M N O P Q R S T U V W X

תש

Y Z

תצצפעףסנמלמככדטיחודהגאב

a b c d e f g h i j k l m n o p q r s t u v

קרזש

w x y z

0123456789$.,:;!?

Type 1 filename: dor_____.afm   TrueType filename: dor_____.ttf

Dot Matrix

ABCDEFGHIJKLMNO
PQRSTUVWXYZ
abcdefghijklmno
pqrstuvwxyz
0123456789&$.,:;!?

Type 1 filename: dotmatrx.afm   TrueType filename: dotmatrx.ttf

ABCDEFGHIJKLMNOPQRST
UVWXYZ

abcdefghijklmnopqrstuvwxyz
0123456789&$.,:;!?

Type 1 filename: dow_____.afm   TrueType filename: dow_____.ttf

Dragonwick

ABCDEFGH
IJKLMNOPQ
RSTUVWXYZ

abcdefghijklmnopqrstuvwxyz
0123456789&$.,:;
!?

Type 1 filename: dragonw_.afm   TrueType filename: dragonw_.ttf

ABCDEFGHIJKLMNOPQR STUVWXYZ
abcdefghijklmnopqrstuvw xyz
0123456789&$.,:;!?

Type 1 filename: dubiel__.afm   TrueType filename: dubiel__.ttf

ABCDEFGHIJKLMNOPQ RSTUVWXYZ
abcdefghijklmnopqrstuvw xyz
0123456789&$.,:;!?

Type 1 filename: dubiel_i.afm   TrueType filename; dubiel_i.ttf

ABCDEFGhIJKLMNO
pqRSTUVWXYZ
ABCDEFGhIJKLMNOpq
RSTUVWXYZ
0123456789&$.,:;!?

Type 1 filename: dublin__.afm   TrueType filename: dublin__.ttf

Dublin Bold

ABCDEFGhIJKLMN
OpqRSTUVWXYZ
ABCDEFGhIJKLMNOp
qRSTUVWXYZ
0123456789&$.,:;!?

Type 1 filename: dublin_b.afm   TrueType filename: dublin_b.ttf

ABCDEFGHIJKLMNO
PQRSTUVWXYZ
ABCDEFGHIJKLMNOPQR
STUVWXYZ
0123456789&$.,:;!?

Type 1 filename: dublinho.afm   TrueType filename: dublinho.ttf

---

Dupuy

ABCDEFGHIJKLMNOPQRS
TUVWXYZ
0123456789&$.,:;!?

Type 1 filename: dupuy___.afm   TrueType filename: dupuy___.ttf

ABCDEFGHIJKLMNOP
QRSTUVWXYZ

ABCDEFGHIJKLMNOPQRSTUVW
XYZ
01234567890

Type 1 filename: dupuyb_b.afm   TrueType filename: dupuyb_b.ttf

Dupuy Balloon Italic

ABCDEFGHIJKLMNOPQRS
TUVWXYZ

ABCDEFGHIJKLMNOPQRSTUVWXYZ
0123456789&$.,:;!?

Type 1 filename: dupuyb_i.afm   TrueType filename: dupuyb_i.ttf

ABCDEFGHIJKLMNOPQRS
TUVWXYZ
0123456789&$.,:;!?

Type 1 filename: dupuy__h.afm   TrueType filename: dupuy__h.ttf

Dupuy Light

ABCDEFGHIJKLMNOPQRS
TUVWXYZ

ABCDEFGHIJKLMNOPQRSTUVW
XYZ

0123456789&$.,:;!?

Type 1 filename: dupuy__l.afm   TrueType filename: dupuy__l.ttf

ABCDEFGHIJKLMNOPQRSTU
VWXYZ

ABCDEFGHIJKLMNOPQRSTUVW
XYZ

0123456789&$.,:;!?

Type 1 filename: durango_.afm   TrueType filename: durango_.ttf

ABCDEFGHIJKLMNOPQ
RSTUVWXYZ
abcdefghijklmnopqrstuvwxyz
0123456789&$.,:;!?

Type 1 filename: eastside.afm   TrueType filename: eastside.ttf

Eileen's Zodiac

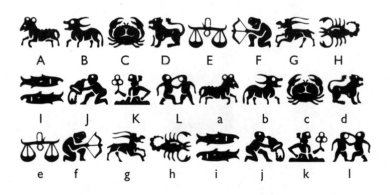

Type 1 filename: eileen__.afm   TrueType filename: eileen__.ttf

ABCDEFGHIJKLM
NOPQRSTUVWXYZ
abcdefghijklmnopqrstuvwxyz
0123456789&$.,:;!?

Type 1 filename: elgar___.afm   TrueType filename: elgar___.ttf

———————————— **Elbjorg Script** ————————————

ABCDEFGHIJKLMNOP
QRSTUVWXYZ
abcdefghijklmnopqrstu
vwxyz
0123456789&$.,:;! ?

Type 1 filename: elbjorg_.afm   TrueType filename: elbjorg_.ttf

Elizabeth Ann

ABCDEFGHIJKLMNO
PQRSTUVWXYZ
0123456789&$.,;:!?

Type 1 filename: elann___.afm   TrueType filename: elann___.ttf

Elzevier-Capitals

Type 1 filename: elzevier.afm   TrueType filename: elzevier.ttf

English Towne

A B C D E F G H I J K L M N O P
Q R S T U V W X Y Z
a b c d e f g h i j k l m n o p q r s t u v w
x y z
0123456789&$.,:;!?

Type 1 filename: englisht.afm   TrueType filename: englisht.ttf

Engraver Light

A B C D E F G H I J K L M
N O P Q R S T U V W X Y
Z A B C D E F G H I J K L M
N O P Q R S T U V W X Y Z
0 1 2 3 4 5 6 7 8 9 & $
. , : ; ! ?

Type 1 filename: engravrl.afm   TrueType filename: engravrl.ttf

Enya

A B C D E F G H J K L M N O P Q
R S T U V W X Y Z
a b c d e f g h i , k l m n o p q r s t u v w
x y z
0 1 2 3 4 5 6 7 8 9 & $. , ; ' ! ?

Type 1 filename: enp_____.afm   TrueType filename: enp_____.ttf

European Courier

Ĭ Ï Į Ǩ Ķ Ĺ Ľ Ļ Ł Ń Ň Ñ Ņ Ò Ó Ő Ô
A B C D E F G H I J K L M N O P Q
Õ Ŏ Ő Ö Ø Ř Ŗ Ś Š Ű Û Ů Ū Ŭ Ü Ų Ý
R S T U V W X Y Z a b c d e f g h
Ÿ Ź Ž Ż
i j k l
Ď Đ È É Ê Ě Ē Ĕ Ë
0 1 2 3 4 5 6 7 8 9

TrueType filename: eurcour.ttf

Faktos

ABCDEFGHIJKLMNOPQR
STUVWXYZ
abcdefghijklmnopqrstu
vwxyz
0123456789&$.,:;!?

Type 1 filename: faktos__.afm   TrueType filename: faktos__.ttf

ABCDEFGHIJKLMNOPQR STUVWXYZ
abcdefghijklmnopqrstu vwxyz
0123456789&$.,:;!?

Type 1 filename: faktos_b.afm   TrueType filename: faktos_b.ttf

ABCDEFGHIJKLMNO
PQRSTUVWXYZ
abcdefghijklmnopqrstuvwxyz
0123456789&$.,:;!?

Type 1 filename: faustus_.afm   TrueType filename: faustus_.ttf

Final Frontier

ABCDEFGHIJKLMNO
PQRSTUVWXYZ
abcdefghijklmnopqrstu
vwxyz
0123456789&$.,:;!?

Type 1 filename: finalfr_.afm   TrueType filename: finalfr_.ttf

FKafka Medium

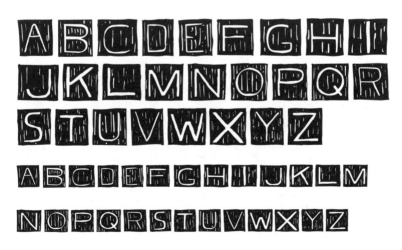

Type 1 filename: fkaf____.afm   TrueType filename: fkaf____.ttf

ABCDEFGHIJKLMNOPQRSTUVWXYZ

abcdefgh ijklmnopqrstuvwxyz

0123456789$..:;!?

Type 1 filename: fletcher.afm   TrueType filename: fletcher.ttf

Fleurons

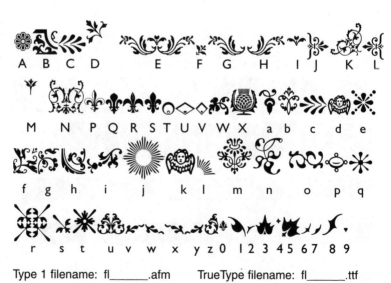

A B C D   E   F G H I J K L

M N P Q R S T U V W X   a b   c d e

f g h   i   j   k   l   m   n   o   p q

r   s   t   u   v   w   x   y z 0 1 2 3 4 5 6 7 8 9

Type 1 filename: fl_____.afm   TrueType filename: fl_____.ttf

Flintstone

ABCDEFGHIJKLMNOPQR
STUVWXYZ
ABCDEFGHIJKLMNOPQRSTUVWXYZ
0123456789&$...::!?

Type 1 filename: flintfon.afm   TrueType filename: flintfon.ttf

Flora

ABCDEFGHIJKLMNOPQR
STUVWXYZ
abcdefghijklmnopqrst
uvwxyz
0123456789&$.,:;!?

Type 1 filename: flora___.afm   TrueType filename: flora___.ttf

ABCDEFGHIJKLMNOPQR STUVWXYZ abcdefghijklmnopqrs tuvwxyz 0123456789&$.,:;!?

Type 1 filename: flora__b.afm   TrueType filename: flora__b.ttf

———— FOOD! ————

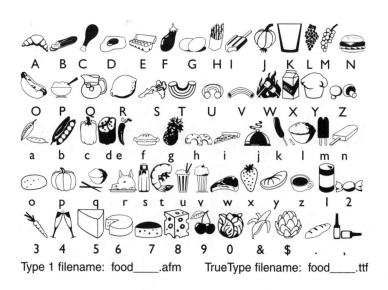

Type 1 filename: food____.afm   TrueType filename: food____.ttf

Fox Script Regular

𝐴𝐵𝐶𝐷𝐸𝐹𝐺𝐻𝐼𝐽𝐾𝐿𝑀𝑁𝑂
𝑃𝑄𝑅𝑆𝑇𝑈𝑉𝑊𝑋𝑌𝑍

abcdefghijklmnopqrstuvwxyz

0123456789&$.,:;!?

Type 1 filename: foxscrip.afm　　TrueType filename: foxscrip.ttf

Frank Ruehl

קצפסנמלכדייטזוהדגבששסללדּוֹ
A B C D E F G H I J K L M N O P Q R S T U V W X
תש
Y Z
שתץצפעפֿסןמלסכדטיחודהגאב
a b c d e f g h i j k l m n o p q r s t u v w
קרז
x y z
0123456789$.,:;!?

Type 1 filename: frankr__.afm　　TrueType filename: frankr__.ttf

קצפסנמלכףייטזוהדגבששללדּוּ
A B C D E F G HI J K LM N O P Q R S T U V W X

תש
Y Z

שתץצפפעסןמלםכדטיחודהגאב
a b c d e f g h i j k l m n o p q r s t u v w

קרז
x y z

0123456789$.,:;!?

Type 1 filename: frankr_b.afm   TrueType filename: frankr_b.ttf

ABCDEFGHIJKLMNOPQ RSTUVWXYZ

abcdefghijklmnopqrstu vwxyz

0123456789&$.,:;!?

Type 1 filename: fruti___.afm   TrueType filename: fruti___.ttf

ABCDEFGHIJKLMNOPQ
RSTUVWXYZ
abcdefghijklmnopqrstu
vwxyz
0123456789&$.,:;!?

Type 1 filename: fruti__o.afm   TrueType filename: fruti__o.ttf

Frutiger Bold

ABCDEFGHIJKLMNOPQ
RSTUVWXYZ
abcdefghijklmnopqrst
uvwxyz
0123456789&$.,:;!?

Type 1 filename: fruti__b.afm   TrueType filename: fruti__b.ttf

ABCDEFGHIJKLMNOP QRSTUVWXYZ
abcdefghijklmnopqrs tuvwxyz
0123456789&$.,:;!?

Type 1 filename: fruti_bo.afm   TrueType filename: fruti_bo.ttf

ABCDEFGHIJKLMNOPQRST UVWXYZ
abcdefghijklmnopqrstuvw xyz
0123456789&$.,:;!"?

Type 1 filename: fruti__c.afm   TrueType filename: fruti__c.ttf

ABCDEFGHIJKLMNOPQ ·
RSTUVWXYZ
abcdefghijklmnopqrstuvw
xyz
0123456789&$.,:;!?

Type 1 filename: fruti_co.afm   TrueType filename: fruti_co.ttf

Frutiger Condensed Bold

ABCDEFGHIJKLMNOPQRST
UVWXYZ
abcdefghijklmnopqrstuvw
xyz
0123456789&$.,:;!?

Type 1 filename: fruti_cb.afm   TrueType filename: fruti_cb.ttf

ABCDEFGHIJKLMNOPQRS
TUVWXYZ
abcdefghijklmnopqrstuv
wxyz
0123456789&$.,:;!?

Type 1 filename: fruticbo.afm   TrueType filename: fruticbo.ttf

—————————— **Frutiger Extra** ——————————

ABCDEFGHIJKLMNO
PQRSTUVWXYZ
abcdefghijklmnopqr
stuvwxyz
0123456789&$.,:;!?

Type 1 filename: fruti__e.afm   TrueType filename: fruti__e.ttf

ABCDEFGHIJKLMNO PQRSTUVWXYZ abcdefghijklmnopqr stuvwxyz 0123456789&$.,:;!?

Type 1 filename: fruti_eo.afm   TrueType filename: fruti_eo.ttf

———————— **Frutiger Extra Bold** ————————

ABCDEFGHIJKLMNO PQRSTUVWXYZ abcdefghijklmnopq rstuvwxyz 0123456789&$.,:;!?

Type 1 filename: fruti_eb.afm   TrueType filename: fruti_eb.ttf

ABCDEFGHIJKLMN OPQRSTUVWXYZ abcdefghijklmnopq rstuvwxyz 0123456789&$.,:;!?

Type 1 filename: frutiebo.afm   TrueType filename: frutiebo.ttf

———————————— **FundRunk** ————————————

ABCDEFGHIJKLMNOPQRSTUVW XYZ abcdefghijklmnopqrstuvwxyz 0123456789&$.,:;!?

Type 1 filename: fundr__r.afm   TrueType filename: fundr__r.ttf

ABCDEFGHIJKLMN OPQRSTUVW
XYZ
abcdefghijklmnopqrstuvwxyz
0123456789&$.,:;!?

Type 1 filename: fundr__i.afm   TrueType filename: fundr__i.ttf

Fusion

ABCDEFGHIJKLMNOPQR
STUVWXYZ
abcdefghijklmnopqrstuvw
xyz
0123456789&$.,:;!?

Type 1 filename: fusion__.afm   TrueType filename: fusion__.ttf

ABCDEFGHIJKLMNOP QRSTUVWXYZ abcdefghijklmnopqr stuvwxyz 0123456789&$.,:;!?

Type 1 filename: fusion_b.afm   TrueType filename: fusion_b.ttf

————————— Marker Felt Thin —————————

ABCDEFGHIJKLMNOPQRSTUV WXYZ abcdefghijklmnopqrstuvw xyz 0123456789&$.,:;!?

Type 1 filename: feltmark.afm   TrueType filename: feltmark.ttf

CIU Gaelach

ᴀbcᴅeꜰʒhıjklmnopqr
sꞇuvɯxyz
ᴀbcᴅeꜰʒhıjklmnopqɲꞃ
ꞇuvɯxyz
0123456789⁊$.,:;!?

Type 1 filename: gaelach_.afm   TrueType filename: gaelach_.ttf

ABCDEFGHIJKLMNOP QRSTUVWXYZ
abcdefghijklmnopqrs
tuvwxyz
0123456789&$.,:;!?

Type 1 filename: galaxy__.afm   TrueType filename: galaxy__.ttf

———————— **Gallaudet** ————————

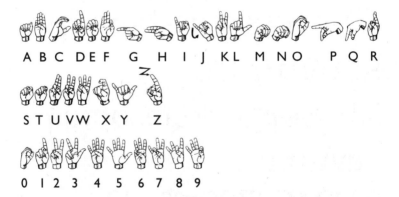

A B C D E F G H I J K L M N O P Q R

S T U V W X Y   Z

0 1 2 3   4   5   6 7 8 9

Type 1 filename: ga_____.afm   TrueType filename: ga_____.ttf

Galledis Medium

ABCDEFGHIJKLMNOPQRSTUVW
XYZ
abcdefghijklmnopqrstuv
wxyz
0123456789€$.,:;!?

Type 1 filename: galledis.afm   TrueType filename: galledis.ttf

Garton Regular

ABCDEFGHIJKLMNOPQR
STUVWXYZ
abcdefghijklmnopqrstuvwxyz
0123456789℧$.,:;!?

Type 1 filename: garton__.afm   TrueType filename: garton__.ttf

ABCDEFGHIJKLMNOPQ
RSTUVWXYZ
abcdefghijklmnopqrstu
vwxyz
0123456789&$.,:;!?

Type 1 filename: genoa__r.afm   TrueType filename: genoa__r.ttf

—————————— Genoa Italic ——————————

ABCDEFGHIJKLMNOPQ
RSTUVWXYZ
abcdefghijklmnopqrstu
vwxyz
0123456789&$.,:;!?

Type 1 filename: genoa__i.afm   TrueType filename: genoa__i.ttf

Geo Plain

ABCDEFGHIJKLMNOPQR
STUVWXYZ
abcdefghijklmnopqrst
uvwxyz
0123456789&$.,:;!?

Type 1 filename: geopla__.afm   TrueType filename: geopla__.ttf

Gessele Script

ABCDEFGHIJKLMNOPQRS
TUVWXYZ
abcdefghijklmnopqrstuvwxyz
0123456789$.,:;!?

Type 1 filename: ges_____.afm   TrueType filename: ges_____.ttf

Gloucester Open Face

ABCDEFGHIJKLMN
OPQRSTUVWXYZ
abcdefghijklmnopqrst
uvwxyz
0123456789&$.,:;!?

Type 1 filename: gloucest.afm   TrueType filename: gloucest.ttf

Goethe

ABCDEFGHIJKLMNO
PQRSTUVWXYZ
abcdefghijklmnopqrstu vwxyz
0123456789&$.,:;!?

Type 1 filename: goethe__.afm   TrueType filename: goethe__.ttf

ABCDEFGHIJKLMNOPQRSTUVW
XYZ
abcdefghijklmnopqrstuvw
xyz
0123456789.,:;!

Type 1 filename: golder__.afm   TrueType filename: golder__.ttf

Good City Modern

ABCDEFGHIJKLMNOPQ
RSTUVWXYZ
abcdefghiiklmnopqrstuvwxyz
0123456789¢$.,:;!?

Type 1 filename: gocmp___.afm   TrueType filename: gocmp___.ttf

ABCDEFGHIJKLMNOPQRS
TUVWXYZ
abcdefghijklmnopqrstuvwxyz
0123456789&.,:;!?

Type 1 filename: goh_____.afm   TrueType filename: goh_____.ttf

Graphic Light

ABCDEFGHIJKLMNOP
QRSTUVWXYZ
abcdefghijklmnopqrstuvw
xyz
0123456789&$.,:;!?

Type 1 filename: graphlig.afm   TrueType filename: graphlig.ttf

ΑΒΧΔΕΦΓΗΙωΚΛΜΝΟΠ
ΘΡΣΤΥηΩΞΨΖ
αβχδεφγηιςκλμνοπθρστυ
αωξψζ
0123456789Ϙϛ.,˙;?

Type 1 filename: greek___.afm   TrueType filename: greek___.ttf

ABCDEFGHIJKLMNOPQRSTU
VWXYZ
0123456789.,˙,˙!?

Type 1 filename: grc_____.afm   TrueType filename: grc_____.ttf

ABCDEFGHIJKLMNOPQRS
TUVWXYZ
abcdefghijklmnopqrstuv
wxyz
0123456789&$.,:;!?

Type 1 filename: greenown.afm   TrueType filename: greenown.ttf

Gregorian HT

ABCDEFGHIJKLMNOP
QRSTUVWXYZ
abcdefghijklmnopqrstu
vwxyz
0123456789&$.,;!?

Type 1 filename: gregorht.afm   TrueType filename: gregorht.ttf

Gregorian Hollow

ABCDEFGHIJKLMNOPQRST
UVWXYZ

abcdefghijklmnopqrstuvwxyz
0123456789&$.:,!?

Type 1 filename: gregorho.afm   TrueType filename: gregorho.ttf

Gresham

ABCDEFGHIJKLMN
OPQRSTUVWXYZ
abcdefghijklmnopq
rstuvwxyz
0123456789&$.,:
;!?

Type 1 filename: gresham_.afm   TrueType filename: gresham_.ttf

Griffin One Dingbats

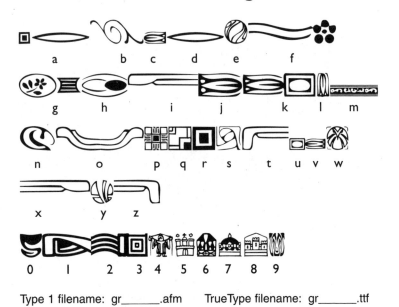

Type 1 filename: gr_____.afm   TrueType filename: gr_____.ttf

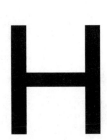

צפסנמלכפךיטזוהדגבשׁשׂלׁדֹךּוֹ

A B C D E F G H I J K L M N O P Q R S T U V W

תשק

X Y Z

ץצףפעןסזמלךכרטיחודהגאב

a b c d e f g h i j k l m n o p q r s t u

קרזשת

v w x y z

0123456789$.,:;!?

Type 1 filename: hadasa_b.afm   TrueType filename: hadasa_b.ttf

──────────────── **Hanch** ────────────────

ABCDEFGHIJKLMNOP

QRSTUVWXYZ

abcdefghijklmnopqrstu

vwxyz

0123456789&$.,:;!?

Type 1 filenaem: hanch___.afm   TrueType filename: hanch___.ttf

ABCDEFGHIJKLMNOP
QRSTUVWXYZ
abcdefghijklmnopqrstu
vwxyz
0123456789&$.,:;!?

Type 1 filename: hanch__i.afm   TrueType filename: hanch__i.ttf

Hanch Bold

ABCDEFGHIJKLMNOP
QRSTUVWXYZ
abcdefghijklmnopqrst
uvwxyz
0123456789&$.,:;!?

Type 1 filename: hanch__b.afm   TrueType filename: hanch__b.ttf

ABCDEFGHIJKLMNOP
QRSTUVWXYZ
abcdefghijklmnopqrst
uvwxyz
0123456789&$.,:;!?

Type 1 filename: hanch_bi.afm   TrueType filename: hanch_bi.ttf

Hancock

ABCDEFGHIJKL
MNOPQRSTUVW
XYZ
abcdefghijklmnopqrstuv
wxyz
0123456789&.,:;!?

Type 1 filename: hancock_.afm   TrueType filename: hancock_.ttf

Handwrite-Inkblot

ABCDEFGHIJKLMNOPQ
RSTUVWXYZ
abcdefghijklmnopqrstuvw
xyz
0123456789&$.,;!?

Type 1 filename: handwrit.afm   TrueType filename: handwrit.ttf

Harquil Roman

ABCDEFGHIJKLMN
OPQRSTUVWXYZ
abcdefghijklmnopqrstu
vwxyz
0123456789.,;!?

Type 1 filename: harquilr.afm   TrueType filename: harquilr.ttf

ABCDEFGHIJKLMNOPQR
STUVWXYZ
abcdefghijklmnopqrstuvw
xyz
0123456789&$.,:;!?

Type 1 filename: harri___.afm   TrueType filename: harri___.ttf

ABCDEFGHIJKLMNO
PQRSTUVWXYZ

ABCDEFGHIJKLMNOPQRSTU
VWXYZ&.,:;!?

Type 1 filename: he_____.afm   TrueType filename: he_____.ttf

Heidelberg

ABCDEFGHIJKLMNOPQ
RSTUVWXYZ
abcdefghijklmnopqrstuvw
xyz
0123456789&$.,:;!?

Type 1 filename: heidelbe.afm   TrueType filename: heidelbe.ttf

Hiragana

りめもやゆよらりるれろわ
A B C D E F G H I J K L

をんあいうえおかけこさし
M N O P Q R S T W X Y Z

すせそたゆってとなにぬね
a b c d e f g h i j k l

のはひふへほまみ
m n o p q r s t

Type 1 filename: hiragana.afm   TrueType filename: hiragana.ttf

Hirosh

ABCDEFGHIJKLM
NOPQRSTUVW
XYZ
0123456789&
$.:;!?

Type 1 filename: hirosh___.afm   TrueType filename: hirosh___.ttf

Hobby Headline

ABCDEFGHIJKLMNOP
QRSTUVWXYZ
abcdefghijklmnopqrstu
vwxyz
0123456789&$.,:;!?

Type 1 filename: hobby___.afm   TrueType filename: hobby___.ttf

ABCDEFGHIJKLMN
OPQRSTUVWXYZ
abcdefghijklmnop
qrstuvwxyz
0123456789&$.,:
;!?

Type 1 filename: holymoly.afm   TrueType filename: holymoly.ttf

Horst Capitals

ABCDEFGHIJKLMN
OPQRSTUVWXYZ
ABCDEFGHIJKLMNOPQRSTU
VWXYZ

Type 1 filename: hoc_____.afm   TrueType filename: hoc_____.ttf

HotDog Medium

ABCDEFGHIJKLMNOPQR
STUVWXYZ
ABCDEFGHIJKLMNOPQRSTUV
WXYZ
0123456789&$.,:;!?

Type TrueType filename: hotdog___.ttf

Hotshot

ABCDEFGHIJKLMNOP
QRSTUVWXYZ
abcdefghijklmnopqrs
tuvwxyz
0123456789&-ſ.,:;!?

1 filename: hotshot_.afm   TrueType filename: hotshot_.ttf

ABCDEFGHIJKLM
NOPQRSTUVWXYZ
abcdefghijklmnopq
rstuvwxyz
0123456789 and $.,.:;!?

Type 1 filename: hspdball.afm   TrueType filename: hspdball.ttf

I

Iglesia Light

ABCDEFGHIJKLMNO
PQRSTUVWXYZ
abcdefghijklmnopqrstubwxyz
0123456789&$.,:;!?

Type 1 filename: iglesia_.afm   TrueType filename: iglesia_.ttf

Inka Bod

ABCDEFGHIJKLMNOPQRSTUVW
XYZ
abcdefghijklmnopqrstuvwxyz
0123456789&$.,:;!?

Type 1 filename: inkabo__.afm   TrueType filename: inkabo__.ttf

Inka Bod Italic

ABCDEFGHIJKLMNOPQRSTUVW
XYZ
abcdefghijklmnopqrstuvwxyz
0123456789&$.,:;!?

Type 1 filename: inkabo_i.afm   TrueType filename: inkabo_i.ttf

Inkwell

ABCDEFGHIJKLMNOP
QRSTUVWXYZ
abcdefghijklmnopqr
stuvwxyz
0123456789&$.,:;!?

Type 1 filename: inkwell_.afm   TrueType filename: inkwell_.ttf

ABCDEFGHIJKLMNOPQRST
UVWXYZ

ABCDEFGHIJKLMNOPQRSTUVWXYZ
0123456789&.,:;!?

Type 1 filename: isado___.afm   TrueType filename: isado___.ttf

J

ABCDEFGHIJKLMNOPQRSTUVW XYZ

abcdefghijklmnopqrstuvwxyz

0123456789&$.,:;!?

Type 1 filename: jana____.afm   TrueType filename: jana____.ttf

──────── Jarrow ────────

ABCDEFGHIJKLMNOPQ RSTUVWXY3

abcdefghijklmnopqrstuvw XY3

0123456789&$.,:;!?

Type 1 filename: jarrow__.afm   TrueType filename: jarrow__.ttf

Jotting

ABCDEFGHIJKLMNOPQR
STUVWXYZ
abcdefghijklmnopqrstuvw
xyz
0123456789&$.,:;!?

Type 1 filename: jor_____.afm   TrueType filename: jor_____.ttf

Jotting Italic

ABCDEFGHIJKLMNOPQ
RSTUVWXYZ
abcdefghijklmnopqrstuvw
xyz
0123456789&$.,:;!?

Type 1 filename: joi_____.afm   TrueType filename: joi_____.ttf

ABCDEFGHIJKLMNOPQ
RSTUVWXYZ
abcdefghijklmnopqrstuv
wxyz
0123456789&$.,:;!?

Type 1 filename: job_____.afm   TrueType filename: job_____.ttf

————— **Jotting Bold Italic** —————

ABCDEFGHIJKLMNOPQ
RSTUVWXYZ
abcdefghijklmnopqrstuv
wxyz
0123456789&$.,:;!?

Type 1 filename: jobi_____.afm   TrueType filename: jobi_____.ttf

Judas Medium

ABCDEFGHIJKLMNOPQRSTUVW
XYZ

ABCDEFGHIJKLMNOPQRSTUVWXYZ
0123456789&$.,:!?

Type 1 filename: judas___.afm   TrueType filename: judas___.ttf

Jumbalaya

ABCDEFGH IJKLMNOPQ
RSTUWXYZ
abCdefghij klmnOpqstuvw
XyZ
0123456789&$.,;:!?

Type 1 filename: jumbal__.afm   TrueType filename: jumbal__.ttf

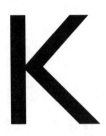

Karloff ―――――

ABCDEFGHIJKLMNOPQRSTU
VWXYZ

ABCDEFGHIJKLMNOPQRSTUVWXYZ
0123456789&:;!?

Type 1 filename: karloff_.afm   TrueType filename: karloff_.ttf

ABCDEFGHIJKLMNOPQRSTUVW
XYZ

abcdefghijklmnopqrstuvwxyz
0123456789¢$.,:;!?

Type 1 filename: kashmir_.afm   TrueType filename: kashmir_.ttf

————————————— **Katakana** —————————————

アイウエオカキクケコサ
A B C D E F G H I J K

シスセソタチツテトナニ
L M N O P Q R S T U V

ヌネノハヘホマミムメモ
W X Y Z c d e f g h i

ヤユヨラリルレロワヲン
j k l m n o p q r s t

Type 1 filename: katakana.afm   TrueType filename: katakana.ttf

ABCDEFGHIJKLMNOPQ RSTUVWXYZ abcdefghijklmnopqrstuv wxyz 0123456789&$.,:;!?

Type 1 filename: kathlita.afm   TrueType filename: kathlita.ttf

ABCDEFGHIJKLMNOPQRSTUVWXY
Z0123456789&.,:;

Type 1 filename: kellne_i.afm   TrueType filename: kellne_i.ttf

ABCDEFGHIJKLMNO
PQRSTUVWXYZ
abcdefghijklmnopqrstuvwxyz
0123456789.,!

Type 1 filename: kellybro.afm   TrueType filename: kellybro.ttf

———— **Kelmscott Medium** ————

ABCDEFGHIJKLMN
OPQRSTUVWXYZ
abcdefghijklmnopqrst
uvwxyz
0123456789&.,:;!?

Type 1 filename: kelmscot.afm   TrueType filename: kelmscot.ttf

ABCDEFGHIJKLMNOPQ
RSTUVWXYZ
abcdefghijklmnopqrstuv
wxyz
0123456789&$.,:;!?

Type 1 filename: kennon__.afm   TrueType filename: kennon__.ttf

ABCDEFGHIJKLMNOPQRSTU
VWXYZ
abcdefghijklmnopqrstuvw
xyz
0123456789&$.,:;!?

Type 1 filename: kennon_i.afm   TrueType filename: kennon_i.ttf

Khachaturian Capitals

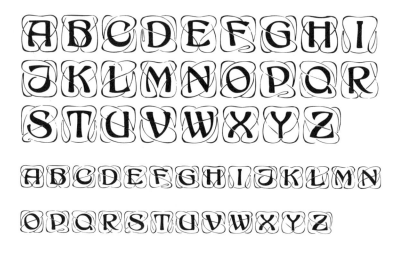

Type 1 filename: khc_____.afm   TrueType filename: khc_____.ttf

Klinzhai Medium

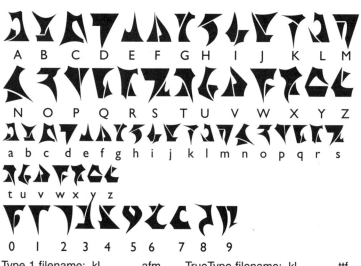

Type 1 filename: kl_____.afm   TrueType filename: kl_____.ttf

ABCDEFGHIJKLMNOPQRSTU
VWXYZ
abcdefghijklmnopqrstuvwxyz
0123456789&.,:;!?

Type 1 filename: kor_____.afm   TrueType filename: kor_____.ttf

Konanur Capitals

ABCDEFGHI
JKLMNOPQR
STUVWXYZ

ABCDEFGHIJKLMN
OPQRSTUVWXYZ

Type 1 filename: kok_____.afm   TrueType filename: kok_____.ttf

Koshgarian Light

ABCDEFGHIJKLMNOP
QRSTUVWXYZ
abcdefghijklmnopqrstu
vwxyz
0123456789&$.,:;!?

Type 1 filename: kol_____.afm   TrueType filename: kol_____.ttf

Kramer

ABCDEFGHIJKLMNOPQR
STUVWXYZ.,:;!?

Type 1 filename: kramer__.afm   TrueType filename: kramer__.ttf

Lancaster

𝕬𝕭𝕮𝕯𝕰𝕱𝕲𝕳𝕴𝕵𝕶𝕷𝕸
𝕹𝕺𝕻𝕼𝕽𝕾𝕿𝖀𝖁𝖂𝖃𝖄
𝖅abcdefghijklmnopqr
stuvwxyz
0123456789&$.,:;!?

Type 1 filename: lancas__.afm   TrueType filename: lancas__.ttf

ABCDEFGHIJKLMNOPQ
RSTUVWXYZ
abcdefghijklmnopqrstuvwxyz
0123456789&$.,:;!?

Type 1 filename: lasrlndn.afm   TrueType filename: lasrlndn.ttf

Lassus Medium

A BCD E F G H I J K LMNO P Q R S T UVW

XY Z a b c d e f g h i j k l m n o p q

r s t u v w x y z 0 1 2 3 4 567 89 0

Type 1 filename: la_____.afm   TrueType filename: la_____.ttf

LED Font HC

ABCDEFGHIJKLMNOPQRSTUVWXY
Zabcdefghijklmnopqrstuvwxyz
0123456789$.,::!?

Type 1 filename: ledfont_.afm   TrueType filename: ledfont_.ttf

Lee Capitals

ABCDEFGHIJKLM
NOPQRSTUVWXYZ
ABCDEFGHIJKLMNOPQRST
UVWXYZ
0123456789&$.,
:;!?

Type 1 filename: leecaps_.afm   TrueType filename: leecaps_.ttf

Lefty Casual

ABCDEFGHIJKLMNOPQ
RSTUVWXYZ
abcdefghijklmnopqrstuvw
xyz
0123456789&$.,:;!?

Type 1 filename: leftycas.afm   TrueType filename: leftycas.ttf

Lemiesz Medium

ABCDEFGHIJKLM
NOPQRSTUVW
XYZ
ABCDEFGHIJKLMNOPQRS
TUVWXYZ
0123456789&.,!?

Type 1 filename: lemiesz_.afm   TrueType filename: lemiesz_.ttf

Libby Script Medium

ABCDEFGHIJKLMNOPQRSTUV
WXYZ
abcdefghijklmnopqrstuvwxyz
0123456789&$.,:;!?

Type 1 filename: libbyscr.afm TrueType filename: libbyscr.ttf

Libra

ABCDEFGHIJKLMNOPQRS
TUVWXYZ
0123456789&$.,:;!?

Type 1 filename: libra___.afm TrueType filename: libra___.ttf

ABCDEFGHIJKLMNOPQRSTUVW
XYZ

ABCDEFGHIJKLMNOPQRSTUVWXYZ

0123456789&.,:;

Type 1 filename: lichtn__.afm   TrueType filename: lichtn__.ttf

Lichtner Italic

ABCDEFGHIJKLMNOPQRSTUVWXYZ

ABCDEFGHIJKLMNOPQRSTUVWXYZ

0123456789&.,:;

Type 1 filename: lichtn_i.afm   TrueType filename: lichtn_i.ttf

aBCDeFGHIJKLm
nopqrstuvwxy
zaBCDeFGHIJKLmn
OPQrsTUVWXYZ
0123456789&$.,:;!?

Type 1 filename: light_bl.afm   TrueType filename: light_bl.ttf

——————— **Light Italic** ———————

ABCDEFGHIJKLMNOPQ
RSTUVWXYZ
abcdefghijklmnopq
rstuvwxyz
0123456789&$.,:;!?

TrueType filename: light__i.ttf

Lightpainter

ABCDEFGHIJKLMNOPQ
RSTUVWXYZ
abcdefghijklmnopqrstuvwxyz
0123456789&$.,:;!?

Type 1 filename: lightpai.afm   TrueType filename: lightpai.ttf

Lilith Light

ABCDEFGHIJKLMNOPQ
RSTUVWXYZ
abcdefghijklmnopqrstuvwxyz
0123456789&$.,:;!?

Type 1 filename: lil_____.afm   TrueType filename: lil_____.ttf

ABCDEFGHIJKLMNOPQ
RSTUVWXYZ
abcdefghijklmnopq
rstuvwxyz
0123456789&$.,:;!?

Type 1 filename: linedraw.afm   TrueType filename: linedraw.ttf

——————————— **Lintsec Medium** ———————————

ABCDEFGHIJKLM
NOPQRSTUVWXYZ
ABCDEFGHIJKLMNOPQRS
TUVWXYZ
0123456789.,:;!?

Type 1 filename: lintsec_.afm   TrueType filename: lintsec_.ttf

LiquidCrystal

RbcdEFGh IJHLⅠnoP9rS
ⅬⅦⅤⅬⅩⅩⅤ2
0 123456789. , : ⌐⁻9P

Type 1 filename: liquidcr.afm   TrueType filename: liquidcr.ttf

Lithograph Black

ABCDEFGHIJKLMN
OPQRSTUVWXYZ

ABCDEFGHIJKLMNOPQRSTU
VWXYZ
0123456789&$.,
:;!?

Type 1 filename: lithogbk.afm   TrueType filename: lithogbk.ttf

ABCDEFGHIJKLMNOPQRSTUVW
XYZ

ABCDEFGHIJKLMNOPQRSTUVWXYZ

0123456789&.,:;

Type 1 filename: li_____.afm   TrueType filename: li_____.ttf

Lombardo Beneventan

abcdefghijklmnopqrstuv
wxyz.,:;!?

Type 1 filename: lombaben.afm   TrueType filename: lombaben.ttf

Lombardoc Medium

ABCDEFGHIJKLMNOPQR
STUVWXYZ

ABCDEFGHIJKLMNOPQRSTUVWXYZ

XIIIIIIIVVVIVIIVIIIIX

Type 1 filename: lo_____.afm   TrueType filename: lo_____.ttf

Longdon Decorative

ABCDEFGHIJKLMNOPQ
RSTUVWXYZ
abcdefghijklmnopqrstuvw
xyz
0123456789&$.,:;!?

Type 1 filename: longdon_.afm   TrueType filename: longdon_.ttf

Loop De Loop Medium

ABCDEFGHIJKLMNOP
QRSTUVWXYZ
ABCDEFGHIJKLMNOPQ
RSTUVWXYZ&.,;:!?

Type 1 filename: loopdelo.afm   TrueType filename: loopdelo.ttf

Lower East Side

ABCDEFGHIJKLMNOP
QRSTUVWXYZ
abcdefghijklmnopqrstu
vwxyz
0123456789&$.,;:!?

Type 1 filename: loes____.afm   TrueType filename: loes____.ttf

ABCDEFGHIJKLMNO
PQRSTUVWXYZ
abcdefghijklmnopqrs
tuvwxyz
0123456789&$.,:;!?

Type 1 filename: lows____.afm   TrueType filename: lows____.ttf

Loxley

ABCDEFGHIJKLMNOPQRSTUVWXYZ
abcdefghijklmnopqrstuvwxyz
0123456789&$.,:;!?

Type 1 filename: loxley__.afm   TrueType filename: loxley__.ttf

LSC Script

ABCDEFGHIJKLMNOPQRSTUVWXY
Zabcdefghijklmnopqrstuvwxyz
0123456789&$.,:;!?

Type 1 filename: lscs____.afm   TrueType filename: lscs____.ttf

Lumparsky

ABCDEFGHIJKLMNOPQ
RSTUVWXYZ
abcdefghijklmnopqrstuvwxyz
0123456789&$.,:;!?

Type 1 filename: lumpa___.afm   TrueType filename: lumpa___.ttf

Luxembourg

abcdefghijklmnopqrsТuvwxyz
abcdefghijklmnopqrstuvwxyz
0123456789&$.,:;!?

Type 1 filename: luxem___.afm   TrueType filename: luxem___.ttf

Toulouse Lautrec

ABCDEFGHIJKLMNOPQRSTUVWXYZ
abcdefghijklmnopqrstuvwxyz
0123456789&$.,:;!?

Type 1 filename: lautrec_.afm   TrueType filename: lautrec_.ttf

Mac Humaine Light

ABCDEFGHIJKLMNOPQRS
TUVWXYZ
abcdefg hijklmnopqrstuvwxyz
0123456789&$.,:;!?

Type 1 filename: machum__.afm   TrueType filename: machum__.ttf

Madrid

ABCDEFGHIJKLMNOPQRSTUVWXYZ

ABCDEFGHIJKLMNOPQRSTUVWXYZ
0123456789$.,:;!?

TrueType filename: madrid__.ttf

Maidstone

ABCDEFGHIJKLMNOPQRSTUVWXYZ

abcdefghijklmnopqrstuvwxyz
0123456789&$.,:;!?

Type 1 filename: maidsscr.afm   TrueType filename: maidsscr.ttf

ABCDEFGHIJLKLMNOPQRSTUVWXYZ

ABCDEFGHIJKLMNOPQRSTUVWXYZ

0123456789&$.,:;!?

TrueType filename: manzanit.ttf

Marbolo

ABCDEFGHIJKLMNOP
QRSTUVWXYZ

ABCDEFGHIJKLMNOPQRSTUVW
XYZ

0123456789&$.,:;!?

Type 1 filename: marbolo_.afm   TrueType filename: marbolo_.ttf

ABCDEFGHIJKLMNOPQRST
UVWXYZ
abcdefghijklmnopqrstuvw
xyz
0123456789&$.,:;!?

Type 1 filename: maft____.afm   TrueType filename: maft____.ttf

MarkerFeltWide-Plain

ABCDEFGHIJKLMNOPQR
STUVWXYZ
abcdefghijklmnopqrstuv
wxyz
0123456789&$.,:;!?

Type 1 filename: mafw____.afm   TrueType filename: mafw____.ttf

MarkerFinePoint-Plain

ABCDEFGHIJKLMNOPQRSTUVWXYZ

abcdefghijklmnopqrstuvwxyz

0123456789&$.,;:!?

Type 1 filename: mafp_____.afm   TrueType filename: mafp_____.ttf

Market Bold

ABCDEFGHIJKLMNOPQR
STUVWXYZ
abcdefghijklmnopqrstuvw
xyz
0123456789&$.,:;!?

Type 1 filename: mkbp_____.afm   TrueType filename: mkbp_____.ttf

Marriage

ABCDEFGHIJKLMNOPQ
RSTUVWXYZ
abcdefghijklmnopqrstuvwxyz
0123456789&$.,:;!?

Type 1 filename: marriage.afm   TrueType filename: marriage.ttf

---------- **Math Symbol** ----------

ABCDEFGHIJKL
MNOPQRSTUV
WXYZ

Type 1 filename: maths___.afm   TrueType filename: maths___.ttf

Mazama

ABCDEFGHIJKLMNOPQRST
UVWXYZ
ABCDEFGHIJKLMNOPQRSTUVW
XYZ
0123456789&$.,:;!?

Mc Garey Fractured

ABCDEFGHIJKLMNOPQ
RSTUVWXYZ
abcdefghijklmnopq
rstuvwxyz
0123456789&.,:;!?

Type 1 filename: mcgf____.afm   TrueType filename: mcgf____.ttf

Memphis Display

ABCDEFGHIJKLMNOP
QRSTUVWXYZ
ABCDEFGHIJKLMNOPQRSTUVW
XYZ

Type 1 filename: memphisd.afm   TrueType filename: memphisd.ttf

Mesozoic Gothic Medium

ABCDEFGHIJKLMN
OPQRSTUVWXYZ
0123456789&.,:;!?

Type 1 filename: mesozic_.afm   TrueType filename: mesozic_.ttf

Miami Beach

ABCDEFGHIJKLMN
OPQRSTUVWXYZ
abcdefghijklmnop
qrstuvwxyz
0123456789&$.,:;!?

Type 1 filename: miami___.afm   TrueType filename: miami___.ttf

Micro Serif Light

ABCDEFGHIJKLMN
OPQRSTUVWXYZ
abcdefghijklmnopqrs
tuvwxyz
0123456789&$.,:;!?

Type 1 filename: mserif__.afm   TrueType filename: mserif__.ttf

ABCDEFGHIJKLMNOP QRSTUVWXYZ

abcdefghijklmnopqrstu vwxyz

0123456789&$.,:;!?

Type 1 filename: milf____.afm   TrueType filename: milf____.ttf

ABCDEFGHIJKLMNOPQ RSTUVWXYZ

abcdefghijklmnopqrstu vwxyz

0123456789&$.,:;!?

Type 1 filename: milf___i.afm   TrueType filename: milf___i.ttf

ABCDEFGHIJKLMNOP
QRSTUVWXYZ
abcdefghijklmnopqrs
tuvwxyz
0123456789&$.,:;!?

Type 1 filename: milf___b.afm   TrueType filename: milf___b.ttf

ABCDEFGHIJKLMNOP
QRSTUVWXYZ
abcdefghijklmnopqrs
tuvwxyz
0123456789&$.,:;!?

Type 1 filename: milf__bi.afm   TrueType filename: milf__bi.ttf

ABCDEFGHIJKLMNOP
QRSTUVWXYZ
abcdefghijklmnopqrstu
vwxyz
0123456789&$.,:;!?

Type 1 filename: milflt__.afm   TrueType filename: milflt_i.ttf

ABCDEFGHIJKLMNOPQ
RSTUVWXYZ
abcdefghijklmnopqrstu
vwxyz
0123456789&$.,:;!?

Type 1 filename: milflt_i.afm

ABCDEFGHIJKLMNOPQR STUVWXYZ
abcdefghijklmnopqrstu vwxyz
0123456789&$.,:;!?

Type 1 filename: milfbk__.afm   TrueType filename: milfbk__.ttf

ABCDEFGHIJKLMNOPQRS TUVWXYZ
abcdefghijklmnopqrstuvw xyz
0123456789&$.,:;!?

Type 1 filename: milfcd__.afm   TrueType filename: milfcd__.ttf

ABCDEFGHIJKLMNOPQRS
TUVWXYZ
abcdefghijklmnopqrstuvw
xyz
0123456789&$.,:;!?

Type 1 filename: milfcd_i.afm   TrueType filename: milfcd_i.ttf

Milford Condensed Bold

ABCDEFGHIJKLMNOPQRS
TUVWXYZ
abcdefghijklmnopqrstuvw
xyz
0123456789&$.,:;!?

Type 1 filename: milfcd_b.afm   TrueType filename: milfcd_b.ttf

ABCDEFGHIJLMNOPQRS TUVWXYZ
abcdefghijklmnopqrstuv wxyz
0123456789&$.,:;!?

Type 1 filename: milfcdbi.afm   TrueType filename: milfcdbi.ttf

—————— Milford Hollow ——————

ABCDEFGHIJKLMNOPQ RSTUVWXYZ
abcdefghijklmnopqrstu vwxyz
0123456789&$.,:;!?

Type 1 filename: milfho__.afm   TrueType filename: milfho__.ttf

ABCDEFGHIJKLM
NOPQRSTUVW
XYZ
abcdefghijklmnop
qrstuvwxyz
0123456789&$.,:;!?

Type 1 filename: mirisch_.afm   TrueType filename: mirisch_.ttf

Monotony Medium

ABCDEFGHIJKLMNOPQRST
UVWXYZ
abcdefghijklmnopqrst
uvwxyz
0123456789&$.,:;!?

Type 1 filename: monot___.afm   TrueType filename: monot___.ttf

Multiform Capitals

ABCDEFGHIJKLMNOPQ
RSTUVWXYZ

ABCDEFGHIJKLMNOPQRSTUVW
XYZ
0123456789.

Type 1 filename: multifor.afm   TrueType filename: multifor.ttf

Musgrave

ᚠᛒ᛿ᛞᛗᚠᛪᚾᛋᛎᚳᚱᛗᛟᚠᚳᚳᛈᚱᛋ
A B C D E F G H I J K L M N O P Q R S

ᚦᚢᛈᚠᚳᛋᛎᛒᛋ
T U V W X Y Z

ᛣᛒᚳᛟᛗᚠᚪᚾᛁᛡᚳᚱᚪᛄᛣᚪᚳᛈᚱᛋᛏ
a b c d e f g h i j k l m n o p q r s t

ᚾᚢᛈᚳᛋᛡᛋ
u v w x y z

TrueType filename: musgrave.ttf

162

Nearsighted

ABCDEFGHIJKLMNO
PQRSTUVWXYZ

ABCDEFGHIJKLMNOPQRSTUV
WXYZ

0123456789&$.,:;!?

Type 1 filename: neone___.afm   TrueType filename: neone___.ttf

NeedlePointSew-Plain

ABCDEFGHIJKLMNO
PQRSTUVWXYZ
abcdefghijklmnopqr
stuvwxyz
0123456789&$.,;"!?

Type 1 filename: neps____.afm   TrueType filename: neps____.ttf

Neon Lights

ABCDEFGHIJKLMNOPQ
RSTUVWXYZ
0123456789 & $.,:;!?

Type 1 filename: neon____.afm   TrueType filename: neon____.ttf

ABCDEFGHIJKLMNOPQ RSTUVWXYZ
abcdefghijklmnopqrstuv wxyz
0123456789&$.,:;!?

Type 1 filename: neuvares.afm   TrueType filename: neuvares.ttf

ABCDEFGHIJKLMN OPQRSTUVWXYZ
abcdefghijklmnopqrstuvwxyz
0123456789&$.,:;!?

Type 1 filename: newborou.afm   TrueType filename: newborou.ttf

ABCDEFGHIJKLMNOPQ
RSTUVWXYZ
abcdefghijklmnopq
rstuvwxyz
0123456789&$.,:;!?

Type 1 filename: newport_.afm   TrueType filename: newport_.ttf

News Gothic

ABCDEFGHIJKLMNOPQRSTU
VWXYZ
abcdefghijklmnopqrstuvw
xyz
0123456789&$.,:;!?

Type 1 filename: newsgo__.afm   TrueType filename: newsgo__.ttf

ABCDEFGHIJKLMNOPQR
STUVWXYZ
abcdefghijklmnopqrstuvw
xyz
0123456789&$.,:;!?

Type 1 filename: newsgo_b.afm   TrueType filename: newsgo_b.ttf

Newtown

ABCDEFGHIJKLMNO
PQRSTUVWXYZ
abcdefghijklmnopqrs
tuvwxyz
0123456789&$.,:;!?

Type 1 filename: newtow__.afm   TrueType filename: newtow__.ttf

ABCDEFGHIJKLMNO PQRSTUVWXYZ
abcdefghijklmnopqrs tuvwxyz
0123456789&$.,:;!?

Type 1 filename: newtow_i.afm   TrueType filename: newtow_i.ttf

Newtown Bold

ABCDEFGHIJKLMN OPQRSTUVWXYZ
abcdefghIJklmnopqr stuvwxyz
0123456789&$.,:;!?

Type 1 filename: newtow_b.afm   TrueType filename: newtow_b.ttf

ABCDEFGHIJKLMNO
PQRSTUVWXYZ
abcdefghijklmnopqr
stuvwxyz
0123456789&$.,:;!?

Type 1 filename: newtowbi.afm   TrueType filename: newtowbi.ttf

NiteClub

ABCDEFGHIJKLMNOPQRSTUV
WXYZ

ABCDEFGHIJKLMNOPQRSTUVWXYZ
0123456789&$.,:;!?

Type 1 filename: niteclub.afm   TrueType filename: niteclub.ttf

ABCDEFGHIJKLMNOPQRSTU
VWXYZ
abcdefghijklmnopqrstuvw
xyz
0123456789&$.,:;!?

TrueType filename: nordic__.ttf

ABCDEFGHIJKLMN
OPQRSTUVWXYZ
abcdefghijklmnop
qrstuvwxyz
0123456789&$.,:
;!?

Type 1 filename: oldbold_.afm   TrueType filename: oldbold_.ttf

ABCDEFGHIJKLMNOPQRSTUVWXYZ
abcdefghijklmnopqrstuvwxyz
0123456789&$.,:;!?

Type 1 filename: oldtwn__.afm   TrueType filename: oldtwn__.ttf

Old Town Condensed

ABCDEFGHIJKLMNOPQRSTUVWXYZ
abcdefghijklmnopqrstuvwxyz
0123456789&$.,:;!?

Type 1 filename: oldtwn_c.afm   TrueType filename: oldtwn_c.ttf

Old Town Extended Regular

ABCDEFGHIJKLMNOPQRSTUVWXY
Zabcdefghijklmnopqrstuvwxyz
0123456789&$.,:;!?

Type 1 filename: oldtwn_e.afm   TrueType filename: oldtwn_e.ttf

קתשקפצצסספמלכיייטוווהחהדדגבבששלדלךון

A B C D E F G H I J K L M N O P Q R S T U V W X Y Z

שתתצצפעוסןןסלמככדטייחווהדדהגאב

a b c d e f g h i j k l m n o p q r s t u v w

קררז

x y z

0123456789$.,:!?

Type 1 filename: ophir____.afm   TrueType filename: ophir____.ttf

―――――――― **Oregon Dry Medium** ―――――――

ABCDEFGHIJKLMNOPQRSTUV WXYZ

abcdefghijklmnopqrstuvw xyz

0123456789&$.,:;!?

Type 1 filename: oregdry_.afm   TrueType filename: oregdry_.ttf

ABCDEFGHIJKLMNOPQRSTUV
WXYZ
abcdefghijklmnopqrstuvw
xyz
0123456789&$.,:;!?

Type 1 filename: oregon__.afm   TrueType filename: oregon__.ttf

Oregon Wet

ABCDEFGHIJKLMNOPQRSTUV
WXYZ
abcdefghijklmnopqrstuvw
xyz
0123456789&$.,:;!?

Type 1 filename: oregwet_.afm   TrueType filename: oregwet_.ttf

ABCDEFGHIJKLMNOP
QRSTUVWXYZ
abcdefghijklmnopqrstuvw
xyz
0123456789&$.,:;!?

Type 1 filename: oswaldgr.afm   TrueType filename: oswaldgr.ttf

Ox Nard

ABCDEFGHIJKLM
NOPQRSTUVW
XYZ

ABCDEFGHIJKLMNOPQR
STUVWXYZ.,;!?

Type 1 filename: oxnard__.afm   TrueType filename: oxnard__.ttf

ABCDEFGHIJKLMNOPQR
STUVWXYZ
abcdefghijklmnopqrstuvw
xyz
0123456789&$.,:;!?

Type 1 filename: oxford__.afm   TrueType filename: oxford__.ttf

Paganini-Lengyar

𝔄𝔅𝕮𝕯𝕰𝔉𝕲𝕳𝕴𝕵𝕶𝕷𝕸
𝕹𝕺𝕻𝕼𝕽𝕾𝕿𝖀𝖁𝖂𝖃𝖄
𝖅abcdefghijklmnopqr
stuvwxyz
0123456789&$.,:;!?

Type 1 filename: paganini.afm   TrueType filename: paganini.ttf

Palladam Medium

ஆறுசுடுஏ ∴.நுஹூ ஈஜ குலு
A   B   C   D   E   F   G   H   I J   K   L

முநுஒபுளுடுஸு துஊள வுஹ
M N O P Q R S   T U V W

ஷ்யுமுஅறசடஎ ˙நுஹுஇஜக
X   Y Z a   b c d e f   g   h   i j k

லமநஒபளரஸ தஉ வருஷயழ
l m n o p q r s   t u   v w x y z

0123456789.,:;!?

Type 1 filename: palladam.afm   TrueType filename: palladam.ttf

177

ABCDEFGHIJKLMNOPQR
STUVWXYZ

abcdefghijklmnopqrstuvwxyz

0123456789&$.,:;!?

Type 1 filename: paradox_.afm   TrueType filename: paradox_.ttf

─────── **Paris Metro** ───────

ABCDEFGHIJKLMNOP
QRSTUVWXYZ

ABCDEFGHIJKLMNOPQRSTUVW
XYZ

0123456789&.,:;!?

Type 1 filename: parismet.afm   TrueType filename: parismet.ttf

Pars Ziba-Draft

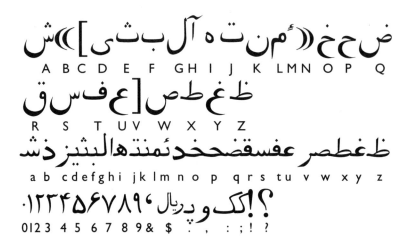

ض ح خ)) (مُ من ت ن م ه آل ب ث ى [((ش

A B C D E F GH I J K LM N O P Q

ظ غ ط ص] ع ف س ق

R S T U V W X Y Z

ظ غ ط ص ر عفسقضحخد ئمنتها البثیر ذش

a b cdefghi jk lm n o p qrs tu v w xy z

۰۱۲۳۴۵۶۷۸۹ ٬ ریال و درپ کک! ؟

0123 4 5 6 7 8 9& $ ٪ ، : ; ! ?

Type 1 filename: parsziba.afm   TrueType filename: parsziba.ttf

---

Partridge - Thin

ABCDEFGHIJKLMNOPQ
RSTUVWXYZ
abcdefgh ijklmnopqrstuvw
xyz
0123456789&$,,,;!?

Type 1 filename: partth_i.afm   TrueType filename: partth_i.ttf

ΛBCDEFGhIJKLⲘNÒ
pqRSⲦUVⲰXYZ

ΛBCDEFGhIJKLⲘNÒpqRSⲦUVⲰXYZ
0123456789&$.,:;!?

Type 1 filename: pceir___.afm   TrueType filename: pceir___.ttf

ABCDEFGHIJKLMNOPQR
SⲦUⅅⅢXYZ

abcdefghijklmnopqrstuvwxyz
0123456789.,:;!?

Type 1 filename: pcmir___.afm   TrueType filename: pcmir___.ttf

PC Ornaments

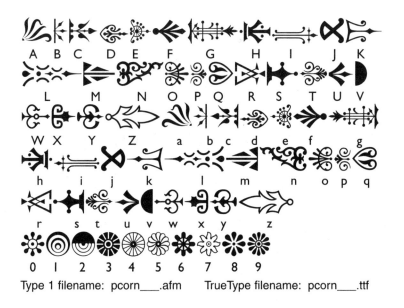

A B C D E F G H I J K
L M N O P Q R S T U V
W X Y Z a b c d e f g
h i j k l m n o p q
r s t u v w x y z
0 I 2 3 4 5 6 7 8 9

Type 1 filename: pcorn___.afm   TrueType filename: pcorn___.ttf

PC Rounders

ꟼBCDEꞓGꞍIꞀꞋLMꞂ
OꟼꝖꝜꓷTUՍꞶXϴƧ

ꟼBCDEꞓGꞍIꞀꞋLMꞂOꟼꝖꝜꞱTUՍꞶ
XϴƧ

0I2Ꝫ꓿ᏕᏮꝛ89 & $. , :;! ?

Type 1 filename: pcrou___.afm   TrueType filename: pcrou___.ttf

ABCDEFGHIJKLMNO PQRSTUVWXYZ

abcdefghijklmnopqrst uvwxyz

0123456789&$.,:;!?

Type 1 filename: pheas___.afm   TrueType filename: pheas___.ttf

Pheasant Italic

ABCDEFGHIJKLMNO PQRSTUVWXYZ

abcdefghijklmnopqrs tuvwxyz

0123456789&$.,:;!?

Type 1 filename: pheas__i.afm   TrueType filename: pheas__i.ttf

ABCDEFGHIJKLMN OPQRSTUVWXYZ abcdefghijklmnopqr stuvwxyz 0123456789&$.,:;!?

Type 1 filename: pheas__b.afm   TrueType filename: pheas__b.ttf

Pheasant Bold Italic

ABCDEFGHIJKLMN OPQRSTUVWXYZ abcdefghijklmnopqrs tuvwxyz 0123456789&$.,:;!?

Type 1 filename: pheas_bi.afm   TrueType filename: pheas_bi.ttf

ABCDEFGHIJKLMNO
PQRSTUVWXYZ
ABCDEFGHIJKLMNOPQRST
UVWXYZ
0123456789&$.,:;!?

Type 1 filename: pheas_sc.afm   TrueType filename: pheas_sc.ttf

ABCDEFGHIJKLMNOPQRS
TUVWXYZ
abcdefghijklmnopqrstuvwxyz
0123456789&$.,:;!?

Type 1 filename: pheast_i.afm   TrueType filename: pheast_i.ttf

Phoenix One

ABCDEFGHIJKLMNOPQRSTUVW
XYZ
abcdefghijklmnopqrstuvwxyz
0123456789&$.,:;!?

Type 1 filename: phoenix1.afm   TrueType filename: phoenix1.ttf

Pig Nose Type Medium

ABCDEFGHIJKLM
NOPQRSTUVWXY
ZabcdEFGHIJklMNOp
qRSTUVWXYZ
0123456789&$.,:;!?

Type 1 filename: pignoset.afm   TrueType filename: pignoset.ttf

Pixel Screen Font Light

ABCDEFGHIJKLMN
OPQRSTUVWXYZ
abcdefghijklmn
opqrstuvwxyz
0123456789&$.,
:;!?

Type 1 filename: pixel___.afm   TrueType filename: pixel___.ttf

Pixie Font Medium

ABCDEFGHIJKLMNO
PQRSTUVWXYZ
abcdefghijklmnopq
rstuvwxyz
0123456789&$.,:;   ?

Type 1 filename: pixiefon.afm   TrueType filename: pixiefon.ttf

Plymouth

ABCDEFGHIJKLMNOPQRSTU
VWXYZ
abcdefghijklmnopqrstuvw
xyz
0123456789&$.,:;!?

Type 1 filename: plymouth.afm   TrueType filename: plymouth.ttf

Polo-Semi Script Medium

ABCDEFGHIJKLMNOP
QRSTUVWXYZ
abcdefghijklmnopqrstuv
wxyz
0123456789&$.,:;!?

Type 1 filename: polo_sem.afm   TrueType filename: polo_sem.ttf

ABCDEFGHIJKLMNO
PQRSTUVWXYZ
ABCDEFGHIJKLMNOPQR
STUVWXYZ
0123456789&$.,:;!?

Type 1 filename: postcry_.afm   TrueType filename: postcry_.ttf

Powell

ABCDEFGHIJKLMNOPQ
RSTUVWXYZ
abcdefghijklmnopqrst
uvwxyz
0123456789$.,;:!?

Type 1 filename: powell__.afm   TrueType filename: powell__.ttf

Powell Italic

ABCDEFGHIJKLMNOPQR
STUVWXYZ
abcdefghijklmnopqrstuv
wxyz
0123456789$.,:;!?

Type 1 filename: powell_i.afm   TrueType filename: powell_i.ttf

Presentor

ABCDEFGHIJKLMNOPQRS
TUVWXYZ
abcdefghijklmnopqr
stuvwxyz
0123456789&$.,:;!?

Type 1 filename: presentr.afm   TrueType filename: presentr.ttf

ABCDEFGHIJKLMNOPQRS
TUVWXYZ
abcdefghijklmnopqrstuvw
xyz
0123456789&$.,:;!?

Type 1 filename: psycho__.afm   TrueType filename: psycho__.ttf

ABCDEFGHIJKLMNO PQRSTUVWXYZ
abcdefghijklmnopqrstu vwxyz
0123456789&$.,:;!?

Type 1 filename: queens__.afm   TrueType filename: queens__.ttf

—————————— **Queen's Park Italic** ——————

ABCDEFGHIJKLMNOP QRSTUVWXYZ
abcdefghijklmnopqrstuvw xyz
0123456789&$.,:;!?

Type 1 filename: queens_i.afm   TrueType filename: queens_i.ttf

ABCDEFGHIJKLMN OPQRSTUVWXYZ abcdefghijklmnopqrs tuvwxyz 0123456789&$.,:;!?

Type 1 filename: queens_b.afm   TrueType filename: queens_b.ttf

——— **Queen's Park Bold Italic** ———

ABCDEFGHIJKLMNO PQRSTUVWXYZ abcdefghijklmnopqrs tuvwxyz 0123456789&$.,:;!?

Type 1 filename: queensbi.afm   TrueType filename: queensbi.ttf

R

FreightIBM

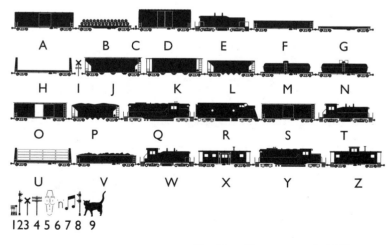

A　　　　B　C　　D　　　E　　　F　　G

H　　I　J　　　K　　L　　M　　N

O　　P　　Q　　R　　S　　T

U　　V　　W　　X　　Y　　Z

123 4 5 6 7 8 9

TrueType filename: rr_frght.ttf

ФИСВУАПРШОЛДЬТЩЗ
A B C D E F G H I J K L M N O P

ЙКЫЕГМЦЧНЯ
Q R S T U V W X Y Z

фисвуапршолдьтщзйкыег
a b c d e f g h i j k l m n o p q r s t u

мцчня
v w x y z

?Øℓ–/;:,.—
0 1 2 3 4 56789

Type 1 filename: russbas_.afm   TrueType filename: russbas_.ttf

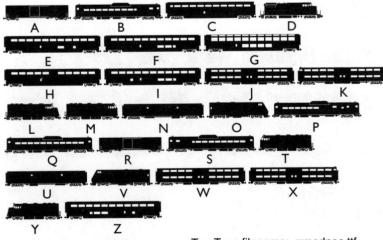

A B C D
E F G
H I J K
L M N O P
Q R S T
U V W X
Y Z

TrueType filename: rrmodpas.ttf

Passenger

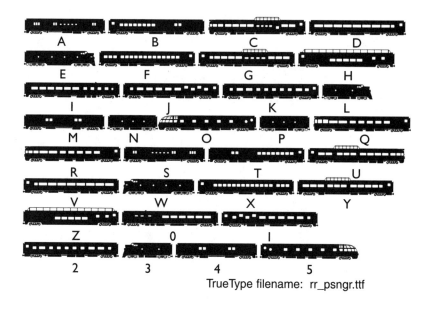

TrueType filename: rr_psngr.ttf

Rabbit Ears

abcdefghijklmnopqrstuvwxyz

abcdefghijklmnopqrstuvwxyz

0123456789&$.,::!?

Type 1 filename: rae_____.afm   TrueType filename: rae_____.ttf

ABCDEF G H IJKLM N NO
P QRST U V W XY Z
a b c d e f g h i j k l m n o p q r s t
u V w x y z
1 2 3 4 5 6 7 8 9 & $. , . ¡ ! ?

Type 1 filename: ransonot.afm   TrueType filename: ransonot.ttf

ABCDEFGHIJKLM
NOPQRSTUVW
XYZ
abcdefghijklmnopqr
stuvwxyz

Type 1 filename: ravennat.afm

Recycle Medium

| A | B | C | D | E | F | J |

Type 1 filename: recycle_.afm   TrueType filename: recycle_.ttf

Red Letter

ABCDEFGHIJKLMNO
PQRSTUVWXYZ
ABCDEFGHIJKLMNOPQRS
TUVWXYZ
0123456789&$.,:;!?

Type 1 filename: redlette.afm   TrueType filename: redlette.ttf

Relief Deco

ABCDEFGHIJKLMNOPQ
RSTUVWXYZ
0123456789&$.,:;!?

Type 1 filename: relief__.afm   TrueType filename: relief__.ttf

Reynolds Capitals Medium

ABCDEFGHIJKLMNOPQRSTUV
WXYZ

ABCDEFGHIJKLMNOPQRSTUVWXYZ.

Type 1 filename: reynocap.afm   TrueType filename: reynocap.ttf

$\mathcal{A} \mathcal{B} \mathcal{C} \mathcal{D} \mathcal{E} \mathcal{F} \mathcal{G} \mathcal{H} \mathcal{I} \mathcal{J} \mathcal{K}$

$\mathcal{L} \mathcal{M} \mathcal{N} \mathcal{O} \mathcal{P} \mathcal{Q} \mathcal{R} \mathcal{S} \mathcal{T} \mathcal{U}$

$\mathcal{V} \mathcal{W} \mathcal{X} \mathcal{Y} \mathcal{Z}$

abcdefghijklmnopqrstuvwxyz

0123456789 & $.,:;!?

Type 1 filename: ricmurry.afm   TrueType filename: ricmurry.ttf

--------- **Riverside** ----------

ABCDEFGHIJKLMNOPQ

RSTUVWXYZ

abcdefghijklmnopqrstuvwxyz

0123456789.!?

Type 1 filename: river___.afm   TrueType filename: river___.ttf

ABCDEFGHIJKLMN
OPQRSTUVWXYZ
abcdefghijklmnopqrstu
uwxyz
0123456789&$.,:;!?

Type 1 filename: rocheste.afm   TrueType filename: rocheste.ttf

Rockmaker

ABCDEFGHIJKLMNO
PQRSTUVWXYZ
0123456789$.,:;!?

Type 1 filename: rockmake.afm   TrueType filename: rockmake.ttf

ABCDEFGHIJKLMNOPQ RSTUVWXYZ abcdefghijklmnopqrstu vwxyz 0123456789&$.,:;!?

Type 1 filename: roissy__.afm   TrueType filename: roissy__.ttf

---------- **Roissy Bold** ----------

ABCDEFGHIJKLMNOPQ RSTUVWXYZ abcdefghijklmnopqrstu vwxyz 0123456789&$.,:;!?

Type 1 filename: roissy_b.afm   TrueType filename: roissy_b.ttf

ABCDEFGHIJKLM
NOPQRSTUVW
XYZ
abcdefghijklmnopqrstuv
wxyz
0123456789&$.,:;!?

Type 1 filename: romeo___.afm   TrueType filename: romeo___.ttf

—————————— **Romulus** ——————————

A B C D E F G H I J K L M N O P Q R

S T U V W X Y Z

a b c d e f g h i j k l m n o p q r s t u v w x y z

Type 1 filename: romulus_.afm   TrueType filename: romulus_.ttf

Roost Heavy

ABCDEFGHIJKLMNOPQ
RSTUVWXYZ
abcdefghijklmnopqrst
uvwxyz
0123456789&$.,:;!?

Type 1 filename: roosthea.afm   TrueType filename: roosthea.ttf

Rothman

ABCDEFGHIJKLMNOPQRSTUVWXYZ

ABCDEFGHIJKLMNOPQRSTUVWXYZ
0123456789

Type 1 filename: rothman_.afm   TrueType filename: rothman_.ttf

Rounded Relief

ABCDEFGHIJKLMNOPQRSTUV
WXYZ
0123456789&$.,:;!?

Type 1 filename: ror_____.afm   TrueType filename: ror_____.ttf

Rounders

ABCDEFGHIJKLMN
OPQRSTUVW
XYZ

ABCDEFGHIJKLMNOPQRSTUV
WXYZ
0123456789&$.,:;! ?

Type 1 filename: rop_____.afm   TrueType filename: rop_____.ttf

RR Key Capitals

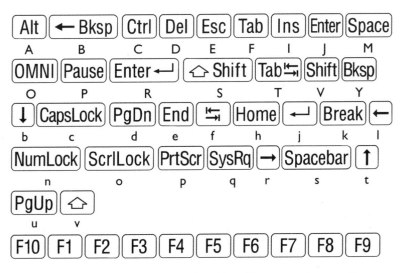

Type 1 filename: rrkeycap.afm   TrueType filename: rrkeycap.ttf

RR Key Capitals Limited

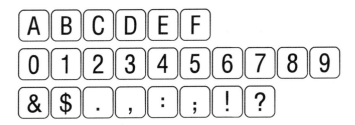

Type 1 filename: rrkeylim.afm   TrueType filename: rrkeylim.ttf

Rudelsberg Medium

ABCDEFGHIJKLMNOP
QRSTUVWXYZ
abcdefghijklmnopqrstuvw
xyz
0123456789.,:;!?

Type 1 filename: rudel___.afm   TrueType filename: rudel___.ttf

Runes of Power

1BJⅩⅯMⱽXⱵⅠ◆ⱵⱤMↃⱵⴼNⱵ
A B C D E F G H I J K L M N O P Q

RↃⱵⱵↃPⱵ 个人
R S T U V W X Y Z

1BJⅩⅯMⱽXⱵⅠ◆ⱵⱤMↃⱵⴼNⱵRↃⱵⱵↃP
a b c d e f g h i j k l m n o p q r s t u v w

Y个人
x y z

Type 1 filename: runes1.afm   TrueType filename: runes1.ttf

S

ArrowFont

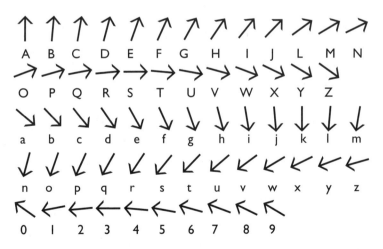

Type 1 filename: sedarrow.afm   TrueType filename: sedarrow.ttf

Saloon Extended

ABCDEFGHIJKL
MNOPQRSTUV
WXYZ
0123456789&$.,:
;!?

Type 1 filename: saloon__.afm   TrueType filename: saloon__.ttf

Salter Medium

ABCDEFGHIJKLMNOPQR
STUVWXYZ

ABCDEFGHIJKLMNOPQRSTUVWXYZ
0123456789&.,;!?

Type 1 filename: salter__.afm   TrueType filename: salter__.ttf

ABCDEFGHIJKLMNOPQ
RSTUVWXYZ
abcdefghijklmnopqrstu
vwxyz
0123456789&$.,:;!?

Type 1 filename: sapir___i.afm   TrueType filename: sapir____.ttf

Sapir Italic

ABCDEFGHIJKLMNOPQ
RSTUVWXYZ
abcdefghijklmnopqrstu
vwxyz
0123456789&$.,:;!?

Type 1 filename: sapir____.afm   TrueType filename: sapir__i.ttf

Savannah

ABCDEFGHIJKLMNOP
QRSTUVWXYZ

ABCDEFGHIJKLMNOPQRSTUVW
XYZ
0123456789.,:;!?

Type 1 filename: savannah.afm   TrueType filename: savannah.ttf

Schneller Medium

ABCDEFGHIJKLMNO
PQRSTUVWXYZ
abcdefghijklmnopqrstu
vwxyz
0123456789&$.,:;!?

Type 1 filename: schnelle.afm   TrueType filename: schnelle.ttf

ABCDEFGHIJKLMNO
PQRSTUVWXYZ
abcdefghijklmnopqrs
tuvwxyz
0123456789&$.,:;!?

Type 1 filename: schwawal.afm   TrueType filename: schwawal.ttf

—— **Secret Code** ——

P	G	C	c	O	f	g	A	\	N	{	-	e	E	k	S	J
A	B	C	D	E	F	G	H	I	K	J	L	M	N	O	P	Q

+	B	j	]	F	u	M	[	>	2	`	U	5	?	H	/	.
S	T	U	V	W	X	Y	Z	a	b	c	d	e	f	g	h	i

z	V	t	n	W	_	a	I	Q	=	%	r	T	v	4	K	y
j	k	l	m	n	o	p	q	r	s	t	u	v	w	x	y	z

"	1	R	0	h	D	L	7	,	d	(	#	s	$	)	w	:
0	1	2	3	4	5	6	7	8	9	&	$	.	,	:	;	!

Type 1 filename: secretco.afm   TrueType filename: secretco.ttf

Sedimentary Font

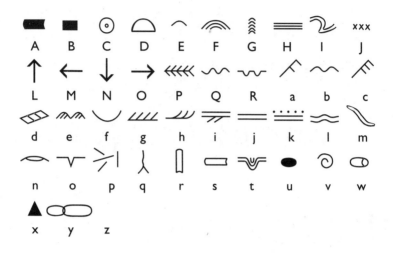

Type 1 filename: sediment.afm   TrueType filename: sediment.ttf

Shoraei Medium

さ	ど	っ	ず	ぐ	ぜ	ぞ	ぶゅや	へ	ぼ	がげ
A	B	C	D	E	F	G	I	M	N	O	Q	R

ざ ど っ ず ぐ ぜ ぞ ぶゅや へ ぼ がげ
A B C D E F G I M N O Q R

し ご び て き ち は だ さ と っ す く せ
S T U V W X Y Z a b c d e f

そ ま ふ ゐ む め ゆ や へ ほ か け し こ
g h i j k l m n o p q r s t

ひ て き ち は た の あ い う え お な に ぬ
u v w x y z 0 1 2 3 4 5 6 7 8

ね ぴ ぇ ん
9 & $.

TrueType filename: shora___.ttf

212

αβçðɛɣGʰɪʲHʒɱɲŋøɵæɾʃθ

A B C D E F G H I J K L M N O P Q R S T

ʊʋʷχʏʒ

U V W X Y Z

abcdefghijklmnopqrstuv

wxyz

Type 1 filename: sildoipa.afm   TrueType filename: sildoipa.ttf

——————————— Silicon-Valley ———————————

ABCDEFGHIJKLMNOPQRST

UVWXYZ

abcdefghijklmnopqrstuv

wxyz

0123456789[.$.,:;!?

Type 1 filename: siliconv.afm

SILManuscript IPA

αβçðɛɣgʰ ɪ ʲ ʜʒɱ̩ŋøøæ

A B C D E F G H I J K L M N O P Q

ɾʃθʊʋʷχʏʒ

R S T U V W X Y Z

abcdfghijklmnopqr

stuvwxyz

Type 1 filename: silmaipa.afm TrueType filename: silmaipa.ttf

SILSophia IPA

αβçðɛɣgʰɪʲʜʒɱ̩ŋøøæɾ

A B C D E F G H I J K L M N O P Q R

ʃθʊʋʷχʏʒ

S T U V W X Y Z

abcdefghijklmnopqrst

uvwxyʒ

Type 1 filename: silsoipa.afm TrueType filename: silsoipa.ttf

ABCDEFGHIJKLMNO
PQRSTUVWXYZ
abcdefghijklmnopqrs
tuvwxyz
0123456789&$.,!?

Type 1 filename: sinaloa_.afm   TrueType filename: sinaloa_.ttf

Slabface

ABCDEFGHIJKLMNOPQR
STUVWXYZ

ABCDEFGHIJKLMNOPQRSTUVWXYZ
0123456789&$.,;;!?

Type 1 filename: slabface.afm   TrueType filename: slabface.ttf

ABCDEFGHIJKLMNOPQRST
UVWXYZ
abcdefghijklmnopqrstu
vwxyz
0123456789&$.,:;!?

Type 1 filename: slantinf.afm   TrueType filename: slantinf.ttf

Slogan

ABCDEFGHIJKL
MNOPQRSTUVWD
XYZ

abcdefghijklmnopqrstuvwxyz
0123456789&$.,:;!?

Type 1 filename: slogan__.afm   TrueType filename: slogan__.ttf

ABCDEFGHIJKLM
NOPQRSTUVWXYZ

ABCDEFGHIJKLMNOPQRST
UVWXYZ
0123456789&$„:;!?

Type 1 filename: snyders_.afm   TrueType filename: snyders_.ttf

SnyderSpeed

ABCDEFGHIJKLM
NOPQRSTUVW
XYZ

ABCDEFGHIJKLMNOPQRST
UVWXYZ
0123456789&$„:;!?

Type 1 filename: snydersp.afm   TrueType filename: snydersp.ttf

Sports and Hobbies

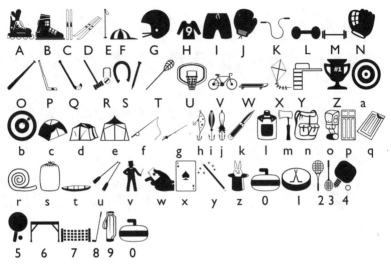

A B C D E F G H I J K L M N
O P Q R S T U V W X Y Z a
b c d e f g h i j k l m n o p q
r s t u v w x y z 0 1 2 3 4
5 6 7 8 9 0

Type 1 filename: sporthob.afm   TrueType filename: sporthob.ttf

Starburst Medium

ABCDEFGHIJKLM
NOPQRSTUVWXYZ

ABCDEFGHIJKLMNOPQRST
UVWXYZ
0123456789$.,;
:!?

Type 1 filename: starb___.afm   TrueType filename: starb___.ttf

Stars & Stripes Medium

ABCDEFGHIJKLMN
OPQRSTUVWXYZ
ABCDEFGHIJKLMN
OPQRSTUVWXYZ
0123456789¢$.,:;!?

Type 1 filename: stars_st.afm   TrueType filename: stars_st.ttf

Steel Plate Gothic

ABCDEFGHIJKLMN
OPQRSTUVWXYZ
ABCDEFGHIJKLMNOP
QRSTUVWXYZ
0123456789&$.,:;!?

Type 1 filename: steel___.afm   TrueType filename: steel___.ttf

ABCDEFGHIJKLMN
OPQRSTUVWXYZ
ABCDEFGHIJKLMNOP
QRSTUVWXYZ
0123456789&$.,:;!?

Type 1 filename: steel__b.afm   TrueType filename: steel__b.ttf

——— **Stick Letter** ———

Type 1 filename: sticl___.afm   TrueType filename: sticl___.ttf

Strongman

ABCDEFGHIJKLM
NOPQRSTUVW
XYZ
ABCDEFGHIJKLMN
OPQRSTUVWXYZ
0123456789&$.,;!?

Type 1 filename: strong__.afm   TrueType filename: strong__.ttf

Strongman Bold

ABCDEFGHIJKLM
NOPQRSTUVW
XYZ
ABCDEFGHIJKLMN
OPQRSTUVWXYZ
0123456789&$.,;!?

Type 1 filename: strong_b.afm   TrueType filename: strong_b.ttf

ABCDEFGHIJKLMN
OPQRSTUVWXYZ
abcdefghijklmnopqrstuvw
xyz
0123456789&$.,:;!?

Type 1 filename: style___.afm   TrueType filename: style___.ttf

---

Stymie

ABCDEFGHIJKLMNOPQ
RSTUVWXYZ
abcdefghijklmnopqrst
uvwxyz
0123456789&$.,:;!?

Type 1 filename: stymie__.afm   TrueType filename: stymie__.ttf

ABCDEFGHIJKLMNOP
QRSTUVWXYZ
abcdefghijklmnopqr
stuvwxyz
0123456789&$.,:;!?

Type 1 filename: swanse__.afm   TrueType filename: swanse__.ttf

Swansea Bold

ABCDEFGHIJKLMNO
PQRSTUVWXYZ
abcdefghijklmnopq
rstuvwxyz
0123456789&$.,:;!?

Type 1 filename: swanse_b.afm   TrueType filename: swanse_b.ttf

ABCDEFGHIJKLMNOP
QRSTUVWXYZ
abcdefghijklmnop
qrstuvwxyz
0123456789&$.,:;!?

Type 1 filename: sydney__.afm   TrueType filename: sydney__.ttf

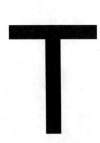

ABCDEFGHIJKLMNO
PQRSTUVWXYZ
abcdefghijklmnopqrstuv
wxyz
0123456789&$.,:;!?

Type 1 filename: tiempo__.afm   TrueType filename: tiempo__.ttf

──────── **NRB Bangkok** ────────

ABCDEFGHIJKLMNOPQRSTU
VWXYZ
abcdefghijklmnopqrstuvwxyz
0123456789&$.,:;!?

TrueType filename: thaibn__.ttf

ABCDEFGHIJKLMNOPQRSTU

VWXYZ

abcdefghijklmnopqrstuvwxyz

0123456789&$.,:;!?

TrueType filename: thaibni_.ttf

———— **NRB Bangkok Bold** ————

ABCDEFGHIJKLMNOPQRST

UVWXYZ

abcdefghijklmnopqrstuvwxyz

0123456789&$.,:;!?

TrueType filename: thaibb__.ttf

ABCDEFGHIJKLMNOPQRST UVWXYZ

abcdefghijklmnopqrstuvwxyz

0123456789&$.,:;!?

TrueType filename: thaibbi_.ttf

Tabatha

ABCDEFGHIJLMNOPQRSTUVWN
TYZ

abcdefghijklmnopqrstuvwxyz
0123456789&$.,:;!?

Type 1 filename: tabatha_.afm   TrueType filename: tabatha_.ttf

ABCDEFGHIJKLMNO
PQRSTUVWXYZ
abcdef ghijklmnopqr
stuvwxyz
0123456789&$.,:;!?

Type 1 filename: tamworth.afm   TrueType filename: tamworth.ttf

Taranis

ABCDEFGHIJKL
MNOPQRSTUV
WXYZ

abcdefgh ijklmnopqrstuvwxyz
0123456789&$.,:;!?

Type 1 filename: taranis_.afm   TrueType filename: taranis_.ttf

ABCDEFGHIJK
LMNOPQRSTUV
WXYZ
abcdefghijklmn
opqrstuvwxyz
0123456789
&$.,:;!?

Type 1 filename: telfor__.afm   TrueType filename: telfor__.ttf

ABCDEFGHIJK
LMNOPQRSTUV
WXYZ
abcdefghijklmn
opqrstuvwxyz
0123456789
&$.,:;!?

Type 1 filename: telfor_i.afm   TrueType filename: telfor_i.ttf

Telford Hollow

ABCDEFGHIJK
LMNOPQRSTUV
WXYZ
abcdefghijklmn
opqrstuvwxyz
0123456789
&$.,:;!?

Type 1 filename: telfho__.afm   TrueType filename: telfho__.ttf

Telford Hollow Italic

ABCDEFGHIJK
LMNOPQRSTUV
WXYZ
abcdefghijklmn
opqrstuvwxyz
0123456789
&$.,:;!?

Type 1 filename: telfho_i.afm   TrueType filename: telfho_i.ttf

ABCDEFGHIJKLMNOP
QRSTUVWXYZ
abcdefghijklmnopqrstuv
wxyz
0123456789&$.,:;!?

Type 1 filename: tempus__.afm   TrueType filename: tempus__.ttf

ABCDEFGHIJKLM
NOPQRSTUVW
XYZ
abcdefghijklmnopqrstu
vwxyz
0123456789.,:;!?

Type 1 filename: th_____.afm   TrueType filename: th_____.ttf

ABCDEFGHIJKLMNOP
QRSTUVWXYZ
abcdefghijklmnopqrstuvw
xyz
0123456789&$.,:;!?

Type 1 filename: times__m.afm   TrueType filename: times__m.ttf

Tiverton

ABCDEFGHIJKLMNOPQRSTUVWXYZ

ABCDEFGHIJKLMNOPQRSTUVWXYZ
0123456789&$.,:;!?

Type 1 filename: tiverton.afm   TrueType filename: tiverton.ttf

Tone and Debs

ABCDEFGHIJKLMNOPQR
STUVWXYZ

ABCDEFGHIJKLMNOPQRSTUVWXYZ
0123456789&$.,;;!?

Type 1 filename: tone____.afm   TrueType filename: tone____.ttf

Toy Block Medium

ABCDEFGH I JI I M
OPOPSTUVWXYZ
ABCDEFGHIJKLMN
OPQRSTUVWXYZ
0123456789&$.,
:;!?

Type 1 filename: toyblock.afm   TrueType filename: toyblock.ttf

Trains

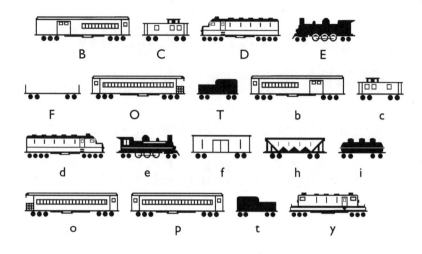

Type 1 filename: trains_ .afm   TrueType filename: trains__.ttf

Trajanus Roman

ABCDEFGHIJKLMN
OPQRSTUVWXYZ

ABCDEFGHIJKLMNOPQRST
UVWXYZ
0123456789&$.,: ;!?

Type 1 filename: trajanus.afm   TrueType filename: trajanus.ttf

ABCDEFGHIJKLMN
OPQRSTUVWXYZ

ABCDEFGHIJKLMNOPQRSTU

VWXYZ

0123456789&$.,:;!?

Type 1 filename: tribeca_.afm   TrueType filename: tribeca_.ttf

Two Griffin

ABCDEFGHIJKLM
NOPQRSTUVW
XYZ

Type 1 filename: tw_____.afm   TrueType filename: tw_____.ttf

U

𝕬𝕭𝕮𝕯𝕰𝕱𝕲𝕳𝕴𝕵𝕶𝕷𝕸𝕹
𝕺𝕻𝕼𝕽𝕾𝕿𝖀𝖁𝖂𝖃𝖄𝖅
abcdefghijklmnopqrstuvwxyz
0123456789&$.,:;!?

Type 1 filename: ueg_____.afm   TrueType filename: ueg_____.ttf

ABCDEFGHIJKLMN OPQRSTUVWXYZ abcdefghijklmnop qrstuvwxyz 0123456789&$.,:;!?

Type 1 filename: ultrabla.afm   TrueType filename: ultrabla.ttf

Uncia Dis Medium

ABCDEFGHIJKLMNOPQRSTU VWXYZ ABCDEFGHIJKLMNOPQRSTUVW XYZ 0123456789&$.,:;!?

Type 1 filename: unciadis.afm   TrueType filename: unciadis.ttf

HTC5NWBgqQ6YKEAr2
A B C D E F G H I J L M N O P Q R

Pvdkn[{}
S T U V W X Y Z

p%D9MFG4'UO-*m?)+
a b c d e f g h i j k l m n o p q

u.lXw;/zj
r s t u v w x y z

31b`xe<7~"R,i8!>(
0 1 2 3 4 5 6 7 8 9 & $. , : ; !

Type 1 filename: uncodsec.afm   TrueType filename: uncodsec.ttf

ABCDEFGHIJKLMNOPQRS
TUVWXYZ

abcdefghijklmnopqrstuvwxyz

0123456789&$.,:;!?

Type 1 filename: upes____.afm   TrueType filename: upes____.ttf

ABCDEFGHIJKLMNOPQ RSTUVWXYZ
abcdefghijklmnopqrstuv wxyz
0123456789&$.,:;!?

Type 1 filename: upsil____.afm   TrueType filename: upsil____.ttf

ABCDEFGHIJKLMNO
PQRSTUVWXYZ
abcdefghijklmnopqrst
uvwxyz
0123456789&$.,:;!?

Type 1 filename: utrg_____.afm   TrueType filename: utrg_____.ttf

Utopia Medium Italic

*ABCDEFGHIJKLMNO
PQRSTUVWXYZ
abcdefghijklmnopqrs
tuvwxyz
0123456789&$.,:;!?*

Type 1 filename: uti_____.afm   TrueType filename: uti_____.ttf

ABCDEFGHIJKLMNO
PQRSTUVWXYZ
abcdefghijklmnopqrs
tuvwxyz
0123456789&$.,:;!?

Type 1 filename: utb_____.afm   TrueType filename: utb_____.ttf

Utopia Bold Italic

ABCDEFGHIJKLMNO
PQRSTUVWXYZ
abcdefghijklmnopqrs
tuvwxyz
0123456789&$.,:;!?

Type 1 filename: utbi____.afm   TrueType filename: utbi____.ttf

Vagabond

ABCDEFGHIJKLMNOPQR
STUVWXYZ
abcdefghijklmnopqrstuv
wxyz
0123456789&$.,:;!?

Type 1 filename: vagabond.afm   TrueType filename: vagabond.ttf

Vagabond Hollow

ABCDEFGHIJKLMNOPQRST
UVWXYZ
abcdefghijklmnopqrstuvwxyz
0123456789&$.,:;!?

Type 1 filename: vagab_ho.afm   TrueType filename: vagab_ho.ttf

Vassallo

ABCDEFGHIJKLMNOPQR
STUVWXYZ
abcdefghijklmnopqrstuvw
xyz
0123456789&$.,:;!?

Type 1 filename: vassallo.afm   TrueType filename: vassallo.ttf

Victorias Secret

ABCDEFGHIJKLMNOPQ
RSTUVWXYZ
abcdefghijklmnopqrstuvw
xyz
0123456789&$.,;:!?

Type 1 filename: vis_____.afm   TrueType filename: vis_____.ttf

Video Terminal Screen

ABCDEFGHIJKLMNOPQRS
TUVWXYZ
abcdefghijklmnopqrs
tuvwxyz
0123456789&$.,:;!?

Type 1 filename: video____.afm   TrueType filename: video____.ttf

תשקצפפסנמלכף׳יטזווד׳גב שׁשׁ ללךוֹ

A B C D E F G HI JLMNOPQR S TU VWX Y Z

קרזשׁת׳צפעפפסנמלםכדטיחודהגאב

a b c d e f g h i j k l m n o p q r s t u v w x y z

0123456789$.,:;!?

Type 1 filename: vilna___.afm   TrueType filename: vilna___.ttf

ABCDEFGHIJKLMNOPQRSTUV
WXYZ

abcdefghijklmnopqrstuvwxyz

0123456789&$.,:;!?

Type 1 filename: vireofon.afm   TrueType filename: vireofon.ttf

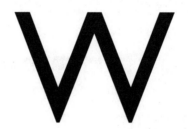

NRB Welsh Gillian

ABCDEFGHIJKLMNOPQ
RSTUVWXYZ
abcdefghijklmnopqrstuvw
xyz
0123456789&$.,:;!?

TrueType filename: wgillr__.ttf

ABCDEFGHIJKLMNOPQRS
TUVWXYZ
abcdefghijklmnopqrstuvw
xyz
0123456789&$.,:;!?

TrueType filename: wgillri_.ttf

───────── **NRB** Welsh Gillian Bold ─────────

ABCDEFGHIJKLMNOP
QRSTUVWXYZ
abcdefghijklmnopqrstuv
wxyz
0123456789&$.,:;!?

TrueType filename: wgillb__.ttf

ABCDEFGHIJKLMNOPQ RSTUVWXYZ
abcdefghijklmnopqrstuv
wxyz
0123456789&$.,:;!?

TrueType filename: wgillbi_.ttf

—— Walrod Initials ——

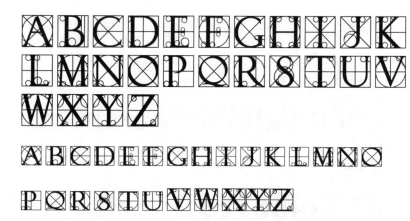

Type 1 filename: walrodin.afm   TrueType filename: walrodin.ttf

Wedgie Medium

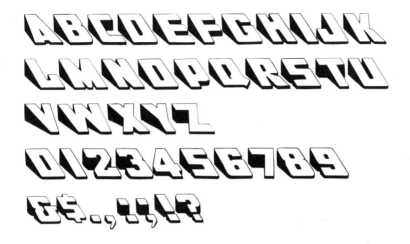

Type 1 filename: wedgie__.afm   TrueType filename: wedgie__.ttf

Weiss

ABCDEFGHIJKLMNOPQR
STUVWXYZ
abcdefghijklmnopqrstuvw
xyz
0123456789&$.,:;!?

Type 1 filename: weiss___.afm   TrueType filename: weiss___.ttf

WestSide Medium

ABCDEFGHIJKLMNOP
QRSTUVWXYZ

ABCDEFGHIJKLMNOPQRSTUVW
XYZ
0123456789&$.,:;!?

Type 1 filename: westside.afm   TrueType filename: westside.ttf

Wharmby

ABCDEFGHIJKLMNOPQRSTU
VWXYZ

ABCDEFGHIJKLMNOPQRSTUVWXYZ
0123456789&$.,:;!?

Type 1 filename: wharmby_.afm   TrueType filename: wharmby_.ttf

Wiltonian Medium

ABCDEFGHIJKLMN
OPQRSTUVWXYZ

ABCDEFGHIJKL MNOPQRSTU
VWXYZ
0123456789&$.,:;!?

Type 1 filename: wilton__.afm   TrueType filename: wilton__.ttf

Wrexham Script

ABCDEFGHIJKLMNO
PQRSTUVWXYZ
abcdefghijklmnopqrstuvw
xyz
0123456789&$.,:;!?

Type 1 filename: wrexham_.afm   TrueType filename: wrexham_.ttf

Yardstick ——————

ABCDEFGHIJKLMNOPQ
RSTUVWXYZ
abcdefghijklmnopqrstuvw
xyz
0123456789&$.,:;!?

Type 1 filename: yards___.afm   Type 1 filename: yards___.afm

ABCDEFGHIJKLMNOPQR STUVWXYZ

abcdefghijklmnopqrstuvwxyz

0123456789&$.,:;!?

Type 1 filename: yards__i.afm   Type 1 filename: yards__i.afm

ABCDEFGHIJKLMNOPQ RSTUVWXYZ

abcdefghijklmnopqrstuvw xyz

0123456789&$.,:;!?

Type 1 filename: yards__b.afm   Type 1 filename: yards__b.afm

ABCDEFGHIJKLMNO
PQRSTUVWXYZ
abcdefghijklmnopqrstu
vwxyz
0123456789&$.,:;!?

Type 1 filename: yoxall__.afm   Type 1 filename: yoxall__.afm

ABCDEFGHIJKLMNO
PQRSTUVWXYZ
abcdefghijklmnopqrstu
vwxyz
0123456789&$.,:;!?

Type 1 filename: yoxall_i.afm   Type 1 filename: yoxall_i.afm

ABCDEFGHIJKLMNO PQRSTUVWXYZ abcdefghijklmnopqrs tuvwxyz 0123456789&$.,:;!?

Type 1 filename: yoxall_b.afm   Type 1 filename: yoxall_b.afm

ABCDEFGHIJKLMNO PQRSTUVWXYZ abcdefghijklmnopqrst uvwxyz 0123456789&$.,:;!?

Type 1 filename: yoxallbi.afm   Type 1 filename: yoxallbi.afm

Z

Zaleski Capitals

ABCDEFGHIJKLM
NOPQRSTUVW
XYZ
ABCDEFGHIJKLMNOPQR
STUVWXYZ
0123456789&$.!?

Type 1 filename: zaleski_.afm   TrueType filename: zaleski_.ttf

Zarrow Medium

Åℬ(◖)ℰ←↑↓↕↔⇄⇅⟋⟍

◎ℙ◉ℝ∑⊤∪⩗⨎)(Ⅴℤ

Åℬℂ𝔇ℰℱℊℍⅡⅉ𝕂ℒℳℕ

⬜ℙℚℝ∑⊤∪⩔ⴸ✕ℽℤ

⊙𝟣ℤℨ𝟦ℾℽℾ𝟪ℽ.ᵧ.⸸⬆ℾ

Type 1 filename: zarrow__.afm   TrueType filename: zarrow__.ttf